# FRENCH
## *in* 3 MONTHS

Ronald Overy and Jacqueline Lecanuet

This edition published in 2016.

First published in the United States
in 2003 by DK Publishing, Inc.,
345 Hudson Street
New York, New York 10014

First published in Great Britain by
Hugo's Language Books Limited

Copyright © 2003 Dorling Kindersley Limited
A Penguin Random House Company

2 4 6 8 10 9 7 5 3 1

ISBN 978-1-46546-269-5

Printed in China

A WORLD OF IDEAS
**SEE ALL THERE IS TO KNOW**

**www.dk.com**

# Preface

*French In Three Months* has been written by two lecturers whose combined experience in teaching French ranges from beginners to graduate level. Both authors taught at the South Bank Polytechnic, now the South Bank University, in London, England, where Jacqueline Lecanuet was Principal Lecturer in French. She is a graduate of Caen and Lille Universities and holds a postgraduate diploma in linguistics. This edition is dedicated to the memory of her late husband Ronald Overy, an inspired teacher and author of textbooks in French, Spanish, and Russian.

The book begins with an explanation of French pronunciation, as far as this is possible in print. If you have bought this book along with the accompanying CDs, these will enable you swiftly to pick up the distinctive sounds of the French language. If not, referring to our system of "imitated pronunciation" will also help you learn to pronounce French accurately and understand it when spoken.

It has always been a principle of our method to teach only what is really essential. We assume that the student wants to learn French from a practical angle; the lessons contain those rules of grammar that will be of most use in this respect. Constructions are clearly explained, and the order in which everything is presented takes into consideration the need for rapid progress. Each week's work includes a large number of exercises and the vocabulary introduced is both practical and up-to-date. Often, in addition to testing a grammatical point, an exercise will include a specific vocabulary, for example: Exercise 45 deals with relative pronouns and the hotel, Exercise 67 with the subjunctive and space travel. The conversations offer examples of everyday French and frequently contain a touch of humor.

The course finishes with a short selection of reading passages illustrating both literary and journalistic styles, all with an English translation. It is important to remember, however, that idiomatic language cannot be translated literally without the occasional appearance of some somewhat stilted phrases.

Ideally, you should spend about an hour a day on your work, although there is no hard and fast rule on this. Do as much as you feel capable of doing; if you have no special aptitude for language-learning, there is no point in forcing yourself beyond your daily capacity to assimilate new material. It is much better to learn a little at a time, and to learn that thoroughly.

Before beginning a new section, always spend ten minutes revising what you learned the day before. Then read each rule or numbered section carefully and reread it to make sure that you have fully understood the grammar, also listening to the CD to pick up the pronunciation of sample sentences and new vocabulary. If you find you are making too many mistakes in the exercises, go back over the section before attempting the same questions again. After you have listened to the Conversations, read them aloud and see how closely you can imitate the voices on the recording.

When the course is completed, you should have a very good understanding of the language—more than sufficient for general vacation or business purposes, and enough to lead quickly into an examination syllabus if this is your eventual aim. Remember that it is important to continue expanding your vocabulary by reading or by watching French films, and best of all, by visiting the country.

We hope you will enjoy *French In Three Months*, and we wish you success with your studies.

# Contents

# Pronunciation

French is a very pleasant sounding language, but it can present English speakers with one or two problems from the point of view of pronunciation.

Hugo's method of imitated pronunciation is sufficiently accurate for you to make yourself understood. Naturally, however, the best way to acquire perfect pronunciation is to practise with the CDs produced to accompany the course. These allow you to hear the words and phrases as you follow them in the book.

Although French spelling may appear complicated, it still remains a better guide to how words are actually spoken than English spelling is.

You should read through the following rules and advice on French pronunciation, but there is no need to learn the rules by heart; just refer back to them at frequent intervals and you will soon become familiar with them.

## STRESS
Unlike English, all syllables in French words are distinctly sounded and evenly stressed, with a little more emphasis being given to the last syllable. Contrast the stress in the word 'important' which appears in both languages:

English: im-POR-tant  French: a*ng*-por-tah*ng*

## PRONUNCIATION OF VOWELS

| | | |
|---|---|---|
| a | is pronounced like 'ah' in English | **la** (the) |
| à | is also pronounced like 'ah' | **là** (there) |
| â | is pronounced like 'ah' but longer | **âne** (donkey) |
| e | in the middle of a syllable is pronounced like ai in 'fair' | **mer** (sea) |
| e | at the end of a syllable is pronounced like er in 'her' | **le** (the) |

| | | |
|---|---|---|
| **e** | is silent at the end of a word | **tasse** (cup) |
| **é** | is pronounced like 'ay' | **été** (summer) |
| **è** | is pronounced like ai in 'fair' | **père** (father) |
| **ê** | is also pronounced like ai in 'fair' | **tête** (head) |
| **i, y** | are pronounced like ee in 'meet' | **ski** (skiing), **y** (there) |
| **o** | is pronounced like o in 'not' | **poste** (post office) |
| **ô** | is pronounced like 'oh' | **hôtel** |
| **u** | this sound does not exist in English; say 'oo' with rounded lips | **vu** (seen) |
| **oi** | is pronounced like 'wah' | **roi** (king) |
| **ou** | is pronounced like 'oo' | **roue** (wheel) |
| **ai, ei** | are pronounced like e in 'let' | **laine** (wool), **reine** (queen) |
| **au, eau** | are pronounced like 'oh' | **au** (to the), **eau** (water) |
| **eu, oeu** | are pronounced like er in 'her' | **neuf** (nine), **soeur** (sister) |

## PRONUNCIATION OF CONSONANTS

French consonants are generally pronounced as in English, but note the following:

| | | |
|---|---|---|
| **c** | before e or i sounds like s | **ceci** (this) |
| **c** | elsewhere sounds like k | **car** (coach) |

| | | |
|---|---|---|
| **ç** | sounds like s | **ça** (that) |
| **ch** | sounds like 'sh' | **château** (castle) |
| **g** | before e or i sounds like s in 'measure' | **général** (general) |
| **g** | elsewhere sounds like g in 'go' | **gare** (station) |
| **h** | is silent | **hôtel** |
| **j** | sounds like s in 'measure' | **je** (I) |
| **qu, q** | sound like k | **qui** (who) |
| **r** | is pronounced at the back of the throat; it is the sound we make when gargling | **rire** (to laugh) |
| **s** | at the beginning of a word sounds like s | **salle** (room) |
| **s** | between two vowels sounds like z | **rose** (rose) |

IMPORTANT With the exception of c, f, l, and r, consonants are not usually pronounced when they form the last letter of a word: **passepor(t)**, **Pari(s)** BUT **hotel**, **professeur**.

## NASAL SOUNDS

These sounds are very characteristic of the French language, but we have nasal sounds in English too: compare: 'sing', 'sang', 'sung', 'song' – remembering that the standard pronunciation gives very little value to the g. French has four very similar nasal sounds, which we show as *ng* in the 'imitatated pronunciation' (see page 12):

| | | |
|---|---|---|
| **om, on** | pronounce like o*ng* in 'song' | **nom** (name), **non** (no) |

| **um\*, un** | pronounce like u*ng* in 'sung' | **un** (one), **brun** (brown) |
|---|---|---|
| **am, an, em, en** | pronounce like 'ah*ng*' | **champ** (field), **an** (year) **temps** (time), **en** (in) |
| **im\*, in, aim, ain, ein** | pronounce like a*ng* in 'sang' | **simple** (easy), **vin** (wine), **faim** (hunger), **bain** (bath), **plein** (full) |
| **ien** | pronounce like 'ee-a*ng*' | **bien** (well) |

\*Some French speakers make no distinction between these two sounds and pronounce them both like a*ng* in 'sang'.

## VARIATIONS

| **er** | at the end of a word of two syllables or more sounds like 'ay' | **parler** (to speak) |
|---|---|---|
| **ez** | at the end of a word sounds like 'ay' | **nez** (nose) |
| **ail** | at the end of a word sounds like 'ah'ee' | **travail** (work) |
| **eil, eille** | sound like 'a'ee' | **soleil** (sun), **bouteille** (bottle) |
| **ill** | usually sounds like 'ee'y' | **billet** (ticket) |
| **gn** | sounds like ni in 'onion' | **signal** (signal) |

## LIAISON

The French like their language to flow smoothly. For this reason, if a word beginning with a vowel or a silent h follows a word ending in a consonant, this consonant is linked to the beginning of the second word:

**nous avons** (noo zah-vo*ng*), we have
**un petit enfant** (u*ng* p'tee tah*ng*-fah*ng*), a small child

When carried over in this way:

**s, x**     sound like z: **deux ans** (der zah*ng*), two years.

**d**     sounds like t: **un grand arbre** (u*ng* grah*ng* tahbr), a tall tree.

**f**     sounds like v: **neuf heures** (ner ve*rr*), nine hours.

## ACCENTS

There are three main accents in French: the acute (**é**), found on the letter e; the grave (**è**), found on a, e and u; the circumflex (**ê**), found on any vowel. There is also the cedilla (**ç**), found only underneath the letter c.

The function of the accents is:

**1** to modify the sound of a letter. The unaccented **e** sounds like er in 'her', the **é** acute sounds like ay in 'say' and the **è** grave sounds like ai in 'fair'.

The **c** which would be hard before an a or o (as in 'car') is softened to sound like s in 'sit' when it has a cedilla added (**garçon**, 'boy').

**2** to distinguish between words having the same spelling but a different meaning. For example, **la** (the), **là** (there); **ou** (or), **où** (where); **sur** (on), **sûr** (sure).

You will find that in French accents are usually not printed when they appear above a capital letter.

## THE IMITATED PRONUNCIATION

Pronounce all syllables as if they formed part of an English word, giving equal stress to each syllable, but note the following:

| | |
|---|---|
| *ng* (italics) | must never be pronounced; these letters merely indicate that the preceding vowel has a nasal sound. |
| e*r* (r italics) | do not pronounce the r; this syllable sounds like er in 'her'. |
| zh | sounds like s in 'measure'. |
| ü | no equivalent in English; round your lips and say 'ee'. |
| o | sounds like o in 'not'. |
| oh | sounds like o in 'note'. |

## THE FRENCH ALPHABET

This is the same as in English, but K and W are not much used. You should know how to pronounce the letters in case you have, for example, to spell out your name to a French receptionist: H-A-L-E-Y sounded as 'ahsh ah el er ee-grek' will make sense to her, the English version would not.

| | | | | | | | |
|---|---|---|---|---|---|---|---|
| **A** | (ah) | **H** | (ahsh) | **O** | (oh) | **V** | (vay) |
| **B** | (bay) | **I** | (ee) | **P** | (pay) | **W** | (doobl-vay) |
| **C** | (say) | **J** | (zhee) | **Q** | (kü) | **X** | (eeks) |
| **D** | (day) | **K** | (kah) | **R** | (airr) | **Y** | (ee-grek) |
| **E** | (er) | **L** | (el) | **S** | (ess) | **Z** | (zed) |
| **F** | (ef) | **M** | (em) | **T** | (tay) | | |
| **G** | (zhay) | **N** | (en) | **U** | (ü) | | |

# Week 1

- *how to say 'the', 'a', and 'some'*
- *how to recognise whether a noun is masculine or feminine, and which article to use with each gender*
- *formation of the plural*
- *how to say 'I', 'you', 'he', 'she', 'it', 'we', 'they'*
- *simple greetings and forms of address*
- *the present tense of 'avoir', 'to have'*
- *formation of the negative*

## 1 ARTICLES: THE, A, AN, SOME

In French all nouns have a gender – they are either masculine or feminine. Articles change depending on the gender of the noun that follows, and whether it is singular or plural.

'The' is expressed by:

| | |
|---|---|
| **le** (masculine singular) | **le passeport** the passport |
| **la** (feminine singular) | **la leçon** the lesson |
| **l'** (before a vowel or h*) | **l'imprimante** the printer |
| | **l'hôtel** the hotel |
| **les** (m. & f. plural) | **les passeports** the passports |

*Note that a few words beginning with h take **le**, **la**.

'A' or 'an' are expressed by:

| | |
|---|---|
| **un** (masculine singular) | **un chéquier** a cheque book |
| **une** (feminine singular) | **une lettre** a letter |

'Some' or 'any' are expressed by:

| | |
|---|---|
| **du** (masculine singular) | **du vin** some wine |
| **de la** (feminine singular) | **de la bière** some beer |
| **de l'** (before a vowel or h) | **de l'alcool** some alcohol |
| **des** (m. & f. plural) | **des leçons** some lessons |

Note: **du** and **des** are both contractions:
**de + le = du;  de + les = des.**

Sometimes 'some' and 'any' are omitted in English, but they must always be expressed in French:

we have wine **nous avons du vin**

## IMITATED PRONUNCIATION (1)

le*r* pahs-porr; lah ler-song; lahl-kol; loh-tel;
lay pahs-porr; u*ng* shek-yay; ün letr; dü va*ng*;
de*r* lah bee-airr; de*r* lahl-kol; day ler-so*ng*;
noo zah-vo*ng* dü va*ng*.

## 2  GENDER OF NOUNS

Unfortunately, there are few rules that can help to determine the gender of French nouns. The best rule of all is to learn each noun and its gender together. Generally speaking, **-e** and **-ion** are feminine endings, although there are exceptions. Nouns denoting male persons are generally masculine and those which refer to female persons are usually feminine:

**le monsieur**  gentleman
**le journal**  newspaper
**le parfum**  perfume
**le château**  castle
**le neveu**  nephew
**le prix**  price
**l'autobus (m.)**  bus

**la dame**  lady
**la valise**  suitcase
**la station**  station

**le journaliste**  male journalist
**la journaliste**  female journalist

Occasionally only one gender exists and this has to be used irrespective of the sex of the person:

**le professeur** (teacher) is always masculine
**la personne** (person) is always feminine

## IMITATED PRONUNCIATION (2)

me*r*s-yer; zhoor-nahl; pahr-fu*n*g; shah-toh; ne*r*-ver; pree; oh-toh-büs; dahm; vah-leez; stahs-yo*n*g; zhoor-nah-leest; pro-fess-e*rr*; pairr-sonn.

## 2A PLURAL OF NOUNS

The plural is formed:

**1** By adding **s**:

**valise** (suitcase) becomes **valises**

**2** By adding **x** to words ending in **au** or **eu**:

**château** (castle) becomes **châteaux**
**neveu** (nephew) becomes **neveux**

**3** By changing the ending **al** to **aux**:

**journal** (newspaper) becomes **journaux**

Words ending in **s** and **x** do not change:

**autobus** (bus or buses); **prix** (price or prices).

## IMITATED PRONUNCIATION (2A)

vah-leez; shah-toh; ne*r*-ver; zhoor-nahl; zhoor-noh; oh-toh-büs; pree.

## Exercise 1

Translate the following:

1 the passport
2 the hotel
3 the suitcase
4 a station
5 a lesson
6 a cheque book
7 a person
8 the journalists
9 the prices
10 some beer
11 some wine
12 some letters
13 some newspapers
14 some buses

## 3  SUBJECT PRONOUNS: I, YOU, SHE, HE, ETC

| singular | | plural | |
|---|---|---|---|
| **je** | I | **nous** | we |
| **tu** | you (familiar) | **vous** | you (familiar) |
| **vous** | you (formal) | **vous** | you (formal) |
| **il** | he, it (m.) | **ils** | they (m.) |
| **elle** | she, it (f.) | **elles** | they (f.) |

Note: **je** becomes **j'** before a vowel or h.

## 3A  ADDRESSING PEOPLE

English, on occasions, can be a very straightforward language. Whether we are addressing a dog, our husband or wife, or our boss, we use the same word 'you'. In French, it's not quite so simple because we have two words for 'you' – **tu** and **vous** – and to use them incorrectly would be a very serious mistake.

The French use **tu** when talking to animals, children, very close friends and relatives. Note, however, that although you use **tu** to one child, you would address more than one child as **vous**. Teenagers use **tu** to each other even on the first meeting.

In all other cases we use the more formal **vous**. Unless we indicate otherwise (by putting in brackets the word 'familiar') we would like you to use **vous** in all the exercises in this book.

Note also that what has been said about **tu** and **vous** also applies to **te** (you), **ton** (your), **votre** (your), etc.

You are no doubt already vaguely familiar with the words **Monsieur**, **Madame**, and **Mademoiselle**; they mean Mr, Mrs, and Miss and are placed, as in English, before a surname:

**Monsieur Dupont, Madame Duval, Mademoiselle Martin.**

The French also use these words a great deal in formal conversation, without a name following:

| | |
|---|---|
| **Bonjour, Monsieur.** | Good morning, good afternoon (to a man). |
| **Bonsoir, Madame.** | Good evening (to a woman). |
| **Au revoir, Mademoiselle.** | Goodbye (to a young woman). |

**Monsieur**, **Madame**, and **Mademoiselle** also have a plural form: **Messieurs**, **Mesdames**, **Mesdemoiselles**.

There is no French equivalent of 'Ms', but these days Madame is increasingly used to address all women, married or otherwise, to avoid any hint of sexism.

# 1

## IMITATED PRONUNCIATION (3, 3A)

zher; tü; voo; eel; el; noo; voo; voo; eel; el; mers-yer
dü-pong; mah-dahm dü-vahl; mahd-mwah-zel
mahr-tang; bong-zhoor, mers-yer; bong-swahr,
mah-dahm; orr-vwahrr, mahd-mwah-zel; mays-yer;
may-dahm; mayd-mwah-zel.

## 4 'AVOIR' (TO HAVE)

This is one of the most important French verbs and it
should be learnt thoroughly.

Present tense
| | |
|---|---|
| **j'ai** | I have |
| **tu as** | you have (familiar sing.) |
| **il a, elle a** | he has, she has |
| **nous avons** | we have |
| **vous avez** | you have (formal, sing. and all pl.) |
| **ils ont, elles ont** | they (m.) have, they (f.) have |

### VOCABULARY

Study these words:
| | |
|---|---|
| **le livre** | book |
| **l'appareil-photo (m.)** | camera |
| **le CD** | CD |
| **la carte** | map, card |
| **la clé** | key |
| **la voiture** | car |
| **la radio** | radio |
| **oui** | yes |
| **non** | no |
| **et** | and |

## IMITATED PRONUNCIATION (4)

ah-vwahr; zhay; tü ah; eel ah; el ah; noo zah-vong; voo
zah-vay; eel zong; el zong; leevr; ah-pah-ray'ee fo-toh;
say-day; kahrt; klay; vwah-tür; rad-yoh; wee; nong; ay.

## Exercise 2

Answer the questions as follows:

Pierre a du vin? Does Pierre have any wine?
Oui, il a du vin. Yes, he has some wine.

**1** Nicole a un journal?

**2** Sophie et Pierre ont une voiture?

**3** Vous avez une radio?

**4** Vous avez une carte?

**5** Nous avons une clé?

**6** J'ai un CD?

## 5   THE NEGATIVE

'Not' is expressed by **ne** placed before the verb and **pas**
after; **ne** becomes **n'** before a vowel or h:

| | |
|---|---|
| **je n'ai pas** | I have not |
| **tu n'as pas** | you have not (familiar sing.) |
| **il n'a pas** | he has not |
| **elle n'a pas** | she has not |
| **nous n'avons pas** | we have not |
| **vous n'avez pas** | you have not (form. sing. and pl.) |
| **ils n'ont pas** | they (m.) have not |
| **elles n'ont pas** | they (f.) have not |

After a negative **un, une, du, de la, de l',** and **des**
change to **de** (**d'** before a vowel or h).

| | |
|---|---|
| **J'ai de la bière.** | I have some beer. |
| **Je n'ai pas de bière.** | I have no beer. |

### IMITATED PRONUNCIATION (5)

zher nay pah; eel nah pah; el nah pah;
noo nah-vong pah; voo nah-vay pah; eel nong pah;
el nong pah; tü nah pah; zhay der lah bee-airr;
zher nay pah der bee-airr.

## Exercise 3

Answer the questions as follows:

Vous avez une voiture? Do you have a car?
Non, je n'ai pas de voiture. No, I don't have a car.

1 Vous avez une valise?
2 Vous avez un passeport?
3 Nous avons du vin?
4 Nous avons un livre?
5 Paul a des CD?
6 Anne-Marie a une radio?
7 J'ai des journaux?
8 Elles ont un appareil-photo?

## Exercise 4

Translate:

1 I have a car.
2 I do not have any keys.
3 We have a suitcase.
4 She has some alcohol.
5 He does not have a newspaper.
6 They (m.) have some books.
7 They (f.) do not have any maps.
8 You do not have a cheque.
9 Do you have a camera?
10 Do you have any CDs?
11 Do you have any books?
12 Do you have a radio?

## VOCABULARY

| | |
|---|---|
| à | at, to |
| au (à + le = au) | at the |
| le contrôle | control, check |
| le policier | policeman |
| l'instant (m.) | moment |
| le miracle | miracle |
| le/la touriste | tourist |
| le portable | mobile phone |
| le baladeur | personal stereo |
| attendez | wait |
| c'est | this is, that is |
| s'il vous plaît | please |
| voici | here is, here are |
| où | where |
| très | very |
| grave | serious |
| peut-être | perhaps |
| mais | but |
| mon Dieu | good heavens |
| aussi | also |

## IMITATED PRONUNCIATION

ah; oh; ko*ng*-trohl; po-lees-yay; a*ng*-stah*ng*; mee-rahkl; porr-tahbl; bah-lah-de*r*; too-reest; say; seel voo play; vwah-see; oo; tray; grahv; kel-ke*r* shohz; may; mo*ng* dyer; oh-see.

## CONVERSATION

*Au contrôle des passeports*

POLICIER **Passeport, s'il vous plaît, Madame.**
TOURISTE **Un instant, s'il vous plaît.**
**[She searches in her handbag.]**
**Le passeport? Où est le passeport? Mon Dieu! J'ai un chéquier, un livre, une carte de France, des clés, un portable, mais ... je n'ai pas de passeport!**
POLICIER **Vous n'avez pas de passeport, Madame? C'est très grave. Mais le passeport est peut-être dans la valise?**
TOURISTE **Attendez, Monsieur.**
**(She searches in her suitcase)**
**J'ai un appareil-photo, un baladeur, et des CD. J'ai aussi du vin, du parfum, un journal ....**
POLICIER **Vous permettez, Madame?**
**[He searches in her suitcase]**
**Voici l'appareil-photo, le journal, le vin, le parfum, le baladeur et les CD. Et ... miracle – voici le passeport!**

## At passport control

OFFICER  Passport please, Madam.

TOURIST  One moment, please.
[She searches in her handbag.]
The passport? Where's the passport? My God!
I've got a cheque book, a book, a map of France,
some keys, a mobile phone, but ... I don't have
a passport!

OFFICER  You've no passport? That's very serious. But
perhaps the passport is in the suitcase?

TOURIST  Wait.
[She searches in her suitcase.]
Yes, I have camera, a personal stereo and some
CDs. I also have some wine, some perfume, a
newspaper ....

OFFICER  May I?
[He searches in her suitcase.]
Here's the camera, the newspaper, the wine, the
perfume, the personal stereo and the CDs. And
... surprise – here's the passport!

# Week 2

- *how to say 'I am', 'you are', etc – the present tense of 'être'*
- *some common adjectives, and how they agree in number and gender with the noun to which they are attached*
- *the present tense of regular verbs ending in '-er'*
- *a variety of ways to frame a question*
- *numbers 0–15*

## 6  'ÊTRE' ('TO BE')

This is another very important verb and should be learned thoroughly.

| | |
|---|---|
| **je suis** | I am |
| **tu es** | you are (familiar sing.) |
| **il est** | he is |
| **elle est** | she is |
| **nous sommes** | we are |
| **vous êtes** | you are |
| **ils sont** | they are (m.) |
| **elles sont** | they are (f.) |

IMITATED PRONUNCIATION (6)
zher swee; tü ay; eel ay; el ay; noo som; voo zet; eel song; el song.

### VOCABULARY

Study these professions:

| | |
|---|---|
| **le médecin** | doctor |
| **le banquier** | banker |
| **le pilote** | pilot |
| **le professeur** | teacher |
| **l'avocat (m.)** | lawyer |
| **l'avocate (f.)** | lawyer |
| **le/la journaliste** | journalist |
| **le/la secrétaire** | secretary |
| **l'astronaute (m. or f.)** | astronaut |

NOTE: When talking about their professions, the French omit the 'a' and say 'I am doctor', 'I am pilot', etc:

**je suis médecin, je suis pilote.**

## IMITATED PRONUNCIATION

med-sa*ng*; bah*ng*k-yay; pee-lot; pro-fess-e*rr*;
ah-vo-kah; ah-vo-kaht; zhoor-nah-leest;
se*r*-kray-tairr; ah-stro-noht.

## Exercise 5

Translate:

1 I am a doctor.
2 He is a pilot.
3 She is a journalist.
4 We are bankers.
5 You (m.) are a lawyer.
6 They (f.) are teachers.
7 They (m.) are astronauts.

## 7 ADJECTIVES

French adjectives have both a masculine and a feminine form, singular and plural. The feminine is normally formed by adding **e** (those already ending in e do not change). In the plural we usually add s:

**Il est intelligent.**  He is intelligent.
**Elle est intelligente.**  She is intelligent.
**Je suis grand.**  I (m.) am tall.
**Je suis grande.**  I (f.) am tall.
**Ils sont petits.**  They (m.) are small.
**Elles sont petites.**  They (f.) are small.

NOTE: The addition of the **e** results in the preceding consonant being pronounced.

Adjectives ending in **x** change the **x** to **se** in the feminine:

**dangereux** (dangerous) becomes **dangereuse**.

## IMITATED PRONUNCIATION (7)

a*ng*-tel-ee-zhah*ng*; a*ng*-tel-ee-zhah*ng*t; grah*ng*; grah*ng*d; p'tee; p'teet; dah*ng*-zher-rer; dah*ng*-zher-rerz.

| VOCABULARY | | | |
|---|---|---|---|
| **riche** | rich | **stupide** | stupid |
| **pauvre** | poor | **poli** | polite |
| **facile** | easy | **impoli** | impolite |
| **difficile** | difficult | **heureux** | happy |
| **intéressant** | interesting | **malheureux** | unhappy |
| **ennuyeux** | boring | **bon, bonne (f.)** | good |
| **intelligent** | intelligent | **mauvais** | bad |

Additional rules for forming the feminine of adjectives:

Final **f** changes to **ve**: **attentif, attentive (f.)** – attentive

Final **er** changes to **ère**: **premier, première (f.)** – first

Final **et** changes to **ète**: **secret, secrète (f.)** – secret

## IMITATED PRONUNCIATION

reesh; pohvr; fah-seel; dee-fee-seel; a*ng*-tay-ress-ah*ng*; ah*ng*-nwee-yer; a*ng*-tel-ee-zhah*ng*; stü-peed; po-lee; a*ng*-po-lee; er-rer; mahl-er-rer; bo*ng*; bonn; moh-vay; ah-tah*ng*-teef; ah-tah*ng*-teev; prerm-yay; prerm-yairr; serkray; serkret.

## Exercise 6

Give the opposite of:

1 Le banquier est riche.
2 La secrétaire est intelligente.
3 Les médecins sont heureux.
4 Les journaux sont intéressants.
5 Le vin est bon.
6 Le livre est facile.
7 L'avocate est polie.
8 La bière est mauvaise.

## 8 REGULAR VERBS ENDING IN -ER

The infinitive (the basic form) of most French verbs ends in **-er**:

| | |
|---|---|
| **préparer** | to prepare |
| **habiter** | to live |
| **travailler** | to work |
| **parler** | to speak |
| **pratiquer** | to practise |
| **regarder** | to watch |
| **écouter** | to listen (to) |

We form the present tense by removing the **-er** from the infinitive and adding:

| | | | |
|---|---|---|---|
| **je** | **-e** | **nous** | **-ons** |
| **tu** | **-es** | **vous** | **-ez** |
| **il/elle** | **-e** | **ils/elles** | **-ent** |

| | |
|---|---|
| **je parle** | I speak |
| **tu parles** | you speak (fam.) |
| **il parle** | he speaks |
| **elle parle** | she speaks |

| | |
|---|---|
| **nous parlons** | we speak |
| **vous parlez** | you speak |
| **ils parlent** | they speak (m.) |
| **elles parlent** | they speak (f.) |

The French **je parle**, **il parle**, etc translates all three forms of the English present tense, i.e. I speak, I do speak, I am speaking.

## IMITATED PRONUNCIATION (8)

pray-pah-ray; ah-bee-tay; trah-vah'ee-yay; pahr-lay; prah-tee-kay; re*r*-gahr-day; ay-koo-tay; zhe*r* pahrl; tü pahrl; eel pahrl; el pahrl; noo pahr-lo*ng*; voo pahr-lay; eel pahrl; el pahrl.

## VOCABULARY

| | |
|---|---|
| **à** | in, at |
| **voyager** | to travel |
| | (**nous voyageons**; see section 81 for details of spelling changes.) |
| **le sport** | sport |
| **la langue** | language |
| **la télévision** | television |
| **la radio** | radio |
| **l'enquête (f.)** | survey |
| **deux** | two |

## IMITATED PRONUNCIATION

ah; vwah-yah-zhay; sporr; lah*ng*g; tay-lay-vee-zee-o*ng*; rahd-yoh; ah*ng*-ket; der.

## Exercise 7

Complete these sentences:

1 Nous (live) à Versailles.
2 Elle (works) à Nice.
3 Il (travels).
4 Je (speak) deux langues.
5 Elles (practise) un sport.
6 Ils (watch) la télévision.
7 Vous (listen to) la radio.
8 Nous (prepare) une enquête.

## 9 ASKING QUESTIONS

In French you can ask a question:

**1** by using a rising intonation – contrast:

**Vous parlez français.** You speak French. (statement)
**Vous parlez français?** Do you speak French? (question)

**2** by using **est-ce que** (**est-ce qu'** before a vowel or h):

**Est-ce que nous travaillons?**
Are we working?
**Est-ce qu'elle écoute la radio?**
Is she listening to the radio?

**3** by putting the pronoun after the verb:

**Voyagez-vous beaucoup?**
Do you travel a great deal?

In this case, if the third person singular of the verb ends in a vowel, a **t** is inserted between it and the pronoun:
**Fume-t-il?** Does he smoke?

Note: 1 and 2 are less formal than 3 and are used more in the spoken language.

## VOCABULARY

| | |
|---|---|
| **téléphoner** | to telephone |
| **réserver** | to reserve |
| **exporter** | to export |
| **importer** | to import |
| **voter** | to vote |
| **inviter à dîner** | to invite to dinner |
| **il y a** | there is, there are |
| **l'hôtel (m.)** | hotel |
| **le directeur** | director |
| **l'ordinateur (m.)** | computer |
| **le président** | the President |
| **la chambre** | bedroom |
| **la voiture** | car |
| **dans** | in |
| **de** | of |
| **en France** | in France, to France |

## IMITATED PRONUNCIATION (9)

frah*ng*-say; ess-ke*r*; boh-koo; füm-teel; tay-lay-fo-nay;
ray-zairr-vay; eks-porr-tay; a*ng*-porr-tay; vo-tay;
a*ng*-vee-tay ah dee-nay; eel yah; oh-tel; dee-rek-te*rr*;
orr-dee-nah-te*rr*; pray-zee-dah*ng*; shah*ng*br; vwah-tür;
dah*ng*; der; ah*ng* frah*ng*s.

## Exercise 8

Using est-ce que, ask your friend whether he/she ...

**1** is telephoning the hotel. (say *to* the hotel)

**2** is reserving a room.

**3** is inviting the director to dinner.

Using a rising intonation, ask about Nicole ...

**4** Is she intelligent?

**5** Is she interesting?

**6** Is she tall?

Using the inverted form, ask about Peter ...

**7** Does he export computers to France?

**8** Does he import cars?

**9** Does he vote for the President?

### 10 NUMBERS

Here are the numbers 0–15:

| | | | |
|---|---|---|---|
| 0 | zéro | 8 | huit |
| 1 | un | 9 | neuf |
| 2 | deux | 10 | dix |
| 3 | trois | 11 | onze |
| 4 | quatre | 12 | douze |
| 5 | cinq | 13 | treize |
| 6 | six | 14 | quatorze |
| 7 | sept | 15 | quinze |

### IMITATED PRONUNCIATION

zay-roh; ung; der; trwah; kahtr; sangk; sees; set; weet, nerf; dees; ongz; dooz; trez; kah-torrz; kangz.

## Exercise 9

Complete the following, writing the answers in words:

a  7 + 2 =        e  10 + 5 =
b  8 − 6 =        f  14 - 2 =
c  3 x 4 =        g  2 x 7 =
d  2 + 3 =        h  2 + 1 =

## VOCABULARY

| | |
|---|---|
| sur | on |
| pour | for |
| beaucoup | a great deal |
| seulement | only |
| souvent | often |
| jamais | never |
| plusieurs | several |
| anglais | English |
| le jogging | jogging |
| l'agence (f.) | agency |
| la publicité | advertising |
| la question | question |
| les affaires (f.) | business |
| faire | to do, to make |

## IMITATED PRONUNCIATION

sürr; poorr; boh-koo; ser*l*-mah*ng*; soo-vah*ng*;
zhah-may; plüz-yerr; ah*ng*-glay; zhog-i*ng*; ah-zhah*ng*s;
pü-blee-see-tay; kest-yo*ng*; ah-fairr; fairr.

# CONVERSATION

*A French radio reporter is preparing a survey on the French. He's interviewing passers-by in the street.*

**2**

JOURNALISTE **Pardon Madame, vous êtes Française?**
PASSANTE **Oui, je suis Française.**
JOURNALISTE **Je prépare une enquête sur les Français. J'ai sept questions.**
PASSANTE **Oui.**
JOURNALISTE **Vous habitez à Paris?**
PASSANTE **Non, j'habite à Versailles.**
JOURNALISTE **Vous travaillez à Paris?**
PASSANTE **Oui, je travaille pour une agence de publicité.**
JOURNALISTE **Est-ce que vous voyagez beaucoup?**
PASSANTE **Oui, je voyage pour affaires.**
JOURNALISTE **Est-ce que vous parlez plusieurs langues?**
PASSANTE **Deux seulement, français et anglais.**
JOURNALISTE **Pratiquez-vous un sport?**
PASSANTE **Oui, je fais du jogging.**
JOURNALISTE **Regardez-vous la télévision?**
PASSANTE **Oui, souvent.**
JOURNALISTE **Vous écoutez la radio?**
PASSANTE **Jamais!**

NOTE: Except when we refer to the people of the country, adjectives denoting nationality do not take a capital letter: 'un hôtel français', 'je parle anglais', but on the other hand 'les Français', the French.

**2**

JOURNALIST   Excuse me Madam, are you French?

PASSER-BY   Yes, I'm French.

JOURNALIST   I'm preparing a survey on the French ... I have seven questions.

PASSER-BY   Yes.

JOURNALIST   Do you live in Paris?

PASSER-BY   No, I live in Versailles.

JOURNALIST   Do you work in Paris?

PASSER-BY   Yes, I work for an advertising agency.

JOURNALIST   Do you travel a great deal?

PASSER-BY   Yes, I travel on business.

JOURNALIST   Do you speak several languages?

PASSER-BY   Only two, French and English.

JOURNALIST   Do you practise a sport?

PASSER-BY   Yes, I go jogging.

JOURNALIST   Do you watch television?

PASSER-BY   Yes, often.

JOURNALIST   Do you listen to the radio?

PASSER-BY   Never!

# Week  3

- *regular verbs ending in '-ir' and their present tense*
- *demonstrative adjectives: this, that, these, those*
- *some useful expressions using 'avoir'*
- *more about negative forms*
- *using question words: where?, when?, how?, etc*
- *the imperative in its simplest form*

**3**

## 11   REGULAR VERBS ENDING IN -IR

The infinitive of a large number of French verbs ends in **-ir**:

| | |
|---|---|
| **finir** | to finish |
| **garantir** | to guarantee |
| **choisir** | to choose |
| **grossir** | to put on weight |
| **maigrir** | to lose weight |
| **remplir** | to fill |
| **réussir** | to succeed |

We form the present tense by removing the **-ir** from the infinitive and adding:

| | | | |
|---|---|---|---|
| **je** | **-is** | **nous** | **-issons** |
| **tu** | **-is** | **vous** | **-issez** |
| **il/elle** | **-it** | **ils/elles** | **-issent** |

| | |
|---|---|
| **je finis** | I finish |
| **tu finis** | you finish |
| **il finit** | he finishes |
| **elle finit** | she finishes |
| **nous finissons** | we finish |
| **vous finissez** | you finish |
| **ils finissent (m.)** | they finish |
| **elles finissent (f.)** | they finish |

NOTE: The singular familiar form **tu finis** should be used only to close friends, children, and animals.

## VOCABULARY

| | |
|---|---|
| **le rapport** | report |
| **le magnétoscope** | video recorder |
| **le gâteau** | cake |
| **le verre** | glass |
| **l'occasion (f.)** | opportunity |
| **saisir** | to seize |

## IMITATED PRONUNCIATION (11)

fee-neerr; gah-rah*ng*-teerr; shwah-zeerr; groh-seerr;
may-greerr; rah*ng*-pleerr; ray-ü-seerr; fee-nee; fee-nee;
fee-nee; fee-nee-so*ng*; fee-nee-say; fee-neess;
rah-porr; man-yay-to-skop; gah-toh; vairr; o-kahz-yo*ng*;
say-zeerr.

## Exercise 10

Translate:

1 I am finishing the report.
2 We guarantee the video recorder.
3 She chooses a cake.
4 He is putting on weight.
5 They (f.) are losing weight.
6 They (m.) are filling the glasses.
7 We seize the opportunity.

## 12 DEMONSTRATIVES: THIS, THAT, THESE, THOSE

Both 'this' and 'that' are expressed by:

| | | |
|---|---|---|
| **ce** (m. sing.) | **ce train** | this/that train |
| **cette** (f. sing.) | **cette voiture** | this/that car |

**ce** becomes **cet** before a vowel or h: **cet hélicoptère**
Both 'these' and 'those' are expressed by:

**ces** (m. & f. pl.)     **ces avions**     these/those planes

If a distinction needs to be made between 'this' and 'that' or 'these' and 'those', we can add **-ci** (short for **ici** 'here') and **-là** ('there') to the noun:

**ce train-ci**     this train
**ce train-là**     that train

## VOCABULARY

| | |
|---|---|
| **le guichet** | ticket office |
| **l'ascenseur (m.)** | lift |
| **le compartiment** | compartment |
| **le billet** | ticket |
| **la gare** | railway station |
| **la place** | seat |
| **rapide** | fast |
| **important** | important |
| **fermé** | closed |
| **cher, chère (f.)** | expensive |
| **plein** | full |
| **réservé** | reserved |
| **occupé** | occupied |
| **valable** | valid |

## IMITATED PRONUNCIATION (12)

ser tra*ng*; set ay-lee-kop-tairr; set vwah-türr; say zahv-yo*ng*; gee-shay; ah-sah*ng*-se*r*r; ko*ng*-pahr-tee-mah*ng*; bee-yay; gahr; plahs; rah-peed; a*ng*-por-tah*ng*; fairr-may; shairr; pla*ng*; ray-zairr-vay; o-kü-pay; vah-lahbl.

## Exercise 11

Translate:

1 This train is fast.
2 This railway station is important.
3 This ticket office is closed.
4 That car is expensive.
5 That lift is full.
6 These seats are reserved.
7 These compartments are occupied.
8 Those tickets are valid.

## 13 USEFUL EXPRESSIONS USING 'AVOIR'

In French there are a number of expressions with **avoir** 'to have' which would be expressed in English with the verb 'to be':

| | |
|---|---|
| **avoir faim** | to be hungry |
| **avoir soif** | to be thirsty |
| **avoir chaud** | to be warm |
| **avoir froid** | to be cold |
| **avoir raison** | to be right |
| **avoir tort** | to be wrong |

**avoir** is also used in connection with age:

**Il a douze ans.** He is twelve. (lit. 'He has twelve years.')

### IMITATED PRONUNCIATION

ah-vwahr fa*ng*; swahf; shoh; frwah; ray-zo*ng*; torr; ah*ng*.

## Exercise 12

Give the opposite of:

**1** Il a raison.

**2** Elle a chaud.

**3** Ils ont tort.

**4** Elles ont froid.

## 14 MORE NEGATIVES: NEVER, NOTHING, ETC

We have already seen that 'not' is expressed by putting **ne (n')** before the verb and **pas** after:

**Je ne travaille pas.** I do not work.
**Il n'écoute pas.** He is not listening.

Here are some more negatives and model sentences:

| | |
|---|---|
| **ne . . . jamais** | never |
| **ne . . . rien** | nothing |
| **ne . . . personne** | no-one |
| **ne . . . plus** | no longer, no more |

**Il ne travaille jamais.** He never works.
**Elle n'exporte rien.** She exports nothing.
**Ils n'invitent personne.** They invite no-one.
**Je ne fume plus.** I no longer smoke.

NOTE
**Rien** and **personne** can also begin a sentence:

**Rien n'est cher.** Nothing is expensive.
**Personne ne fume ici.** No one smokes here.

After a negative **un, une, du, de la, de l', des** change to **de (d')**:

**Je mange de la salade.** I eat salad.
**Je ne mange jamais de salade.** I never eat salad.

## VOCABULARY

| | |
|---|---|
| **la platine laser** | CD player |
| **le fromage** | cheese |
| **l'homme d'affaires** | businessman |
| **la glace** | ice cream |
| **la diététicienne** | dietician |
| **manger** | to eat |
| **rencontrer** | to meet |
| **en** | in, by |

## IMITATED PRONUNCIATION (14)

ne*r*; zhah-may; ree-a*ng*; pairr-sonn; plü; plah-teen lah-zairr; fro-mahzh; om dah-fairr; glahs; dyay-tay-tees-yen; mah*ng*-zhay; rah*ng*-ko*ng*-tray.

## ___ Exercise 13 ___

Answer the questions using 'not', as follows:

Vous voyagez en voiture?   Do you travel by car?
Non, je ne voyage pas en voiture.   No, I don't travel by car.

**1** Vous travaillez?

**2** Vous écoutez?

**3** Vous avez faim?

Now answer using 'never':

**4** Est-ce que vous choisissez du fromage?

**5** Est-ce que vous téléphonez?

**6** Est-ce que vous avez froid?

Now answer using 'nothing':

**7** Mange-t-il une glace?

**8** Prépare-t-elle un rapport?

**9** Exporte-t-il des platines laser?

Now answer using 'no-one':

**10** Nous invitons des hommes d'affaires?

**11** Nous choisissons Paul?

**12** Nous rencontrons la diététicienne?

Now answer using 'no longer':

**13** Est-ce qu'ils ont une voiture?

**14** Est-ce qu'elles habitent à Paris?

**15** Est-ce qu'elles travaillent?

## 15  ASKING: WHERE, WHEN, HOW, ETC

You will need to know how to ask questions in French:

**où?**  where?
**Où est-ce que vous habitez?**  Where do you live?

**quand?**  when?
**Quand écoutez-vous la radio?**
When do you listen to the radio?

**comment?**  how?
**Comment allez-vous?**
How are you? (literally: How do you go?)

**qui?**  who?  whom?
**Qui parle français?**  Who speaks French?
**Qui est-ce qu'elle invite?**  Whom is she inviting?

**pourquoi?**  why?
**Pourquoi téléphone-t-elle?**
Why is she telephoning?

Note the reply to **pourquoi** is **parce que** 'because'.

**quel (m.), quelle (f.)**
**quels (m. pl.), quelles (f. pl.)**  which (what)?

**Quelle chambre réservons-nous?**
Which room are we reserving?

**combien?** how much? how many?
**Combien coûte ce CD?**
How much does this CD cost?
**Combien de fromage désirez-vous?**
How much cheese do you want?
**Combien de trains y a-t-il?**
How many trains are there?

Note: **combien** takes **de (d')** when followed by a noun.

**que** (**qu'** before a vowel) or **qu'est-ce que** what?
**Que mangez-vous?** *or* **Qu'est-ce que vous mangez?**
What are you eating?

Note the word order in the above two questions.

## VOCABULARY

| | |
|---|---|
| **le film** | film |
| **le soir** | evening |
| **l'euro (m.)** | euro |
| **allemand** | German |
| **espagnol** | Spanish |
| **bien** | well |
| **merci** | thank you |
| **chercher** | to look for |

## IMITATED PRONUNCIATION (15)

oo; kahng; ko-mah*ng*; ko-mah*ng* tah-lay voo; kee; poorr-kwah; pahr-sker; kel; ko*ng*-bee-a*ng*; koot; deesk; day-zee-ray voo; yah-teel; ker; kess-ker; mah*ng*-zhay; feelm; swahr; ürroh; ahl-mah*ng*; ess-pan-yol; bee-a*ng*; mairr-see; shairr-shay.

## Exercise 14

Below are ten replies. What were the questions?
The important words are printed in italics.

1 Je travaille *à Paris.*
2 Je regarde le film *ce soir.*
3 *Bien,* merci.
4 *Pierre* téléphone.
5 Ils cherchent *Nicole.*
6 Parce que *j'ai faim.*
7 Je parle *espagnol et allemand.*
8 J'ai *quatre* CD.
9 Ce journal coûte *trois euros.*
10 J'exporte *des magnétoscopes.*

**3**

## 16  THE IMPERATIVE: GIVING ORDERS

On occasions you will need to ask or tell people to do
things. Simply omit the **vous, tu** or **nous** from the
present tense:

| | |
|---|---|
| **Téléphonez.** | Telephone. |
| **Choisissez.** | Choose. |
| **Invitons Paul.** | Let's invite Paul. |
| **Ne téléphonez pas.** | Don't telephone. |
| **N'invitons pas Paul.** | Let's not invite Paul. |

NOTE the final **s** of **-er** verbs is dropped in the familiar
singular imperative:

| | |
|---|---|
| **Choisis.** | Choose. |
| **Finis.** | Finish. |
| **Téléphone.** | Telephone. |

You may wish to add **s'il vous plaît** or **s'il te plaît**
(fam. sing.), meaning 'please', to the imperative.

**3**

### VOCABULARY

| | |
|---|---|
| **les bagages (m.)** | luggage |
| **la méthode** | method |
| **trop** | too much, too many |
| **monter** | to bring up, to take up |
| **acheter** | to buy |

NOTE: **acheter** has a grave accent in the singular and third person plural, which affects pronunciation. See section 81.

| | |
|---|---|
| **j'achète** | **nous achetons** |
| **tu achètes** | **vous achetez** |
| **il/elle achète** | **ils/elles achètent** |

## IMITATED PRONUNCIATION (16)

bah-gahzh; may-tod; troh; mo*ng*-tay; ahsh-tay;
zhah-shet; tü ah-shet; eel ah-shet; el ah-shet;
eel zah-shet; el zah-shet; noo zahsh-to*ng*; voo zahsh-tay.

## ___ Exercise 15 ___

Tell your friend ...

1 ... to reserve two rooms.
2 ... to look for François.
3 ... to seize the opportunity.
4 ... to choose the Hugo method.
5 ... to take up the luggage.
6 ... not to eat too much.
7 ... not to put on weight.
8 ... not to smoke.

And now make some suggestions:

9 Let's speak French.
10 Let's listen to the radio.
11 Let's finish the report.

## VOCABULARY

| | |
|---|---|
| le régime | diet |
| la gymnastique | gymnastics, exercises |
| la chose | thing |
| la vie | life |
| penser | to think |
| je pense que | I think that |
| je dois | I must |
| faire | to do |
| (vous faites) | |
| raccourcir | to shorten |
| chaque | each |
| certain | certain |
| bien | good, fine (as adverb) |
| complètement | completely |
| régulièrement | regularly |
| toujours | always |
| entre | for, between |
| pour | in order to |
| bonjour | good morning, good afternoon |

## IMITATED PRONUNCIATION

ray-zheem; zheem-nah-steek; shohz; vee;
pahng-say; zher pahngs ker; zher dwah; fairr;
voo fet; rah-koor-seerr; shahk; sairr-tang;
bee-ang; kong-plet-mahng; ray-gül-yairr-mahng;
too-zhoorr; ahngtr; poorr; bong-zhoorr.

*Un dialogue entre un homme d'affaires et une diététicienne*

HOMME D'AFFAIRES **Bonjour, Madame.**

DIÉTÉTICIENNE **Bonjour, Monsieur. Un petit instant, s'il vous plaît, je finis ce rapport. Bon. Comment allez-vous?**

HOMME D'AFFAIRES **Je pense que je grossis.**

DIÉTÉTICIENNE **Ah? Vous ne réussissez pas à maigrir? Pourquoi pas?**

HOMME D'AFFAIRES **J'ai toujours faim. J'ai toujours soif. Qu'est-ce que je dois faire?**

DIÉTÉTICIENNE **Faites votre gymnastique régulièrement. Saisissez chaque occasion pour manger de la salade.**

HOMME D'AFFAIRES **Et qu'est-ce que je ne dois pas faire?**

DIÉTÉTICIENNE **Ne choisissez jamais de gâteaux. Ne choisissez jamais de glaces. Ne choisissez jamais de fromage.**

HOMME D'AFFAIRES **Très bien. Et pour le vin?**

DIÉTÉTICIENNE **Ne remplissez jamais votre verre complètement.**

HOMME D'AFFAIRES **Vous garantissez ce régime, Madame?**

DIÉTÉTICIENNE **Oui. Une chose est certaine: si vous grossissez, vous raccourcissez votre vie.**

HOMME D'AFFAIRES **Oui, Madame, vous avez raison.**

*A dialogue between a businessman and a dietician*

BUSINESSMAN  Good morning (Madam).

DIETICIAN  Good morning (Sir). One moment, please, I'll just finish [literally 'I finish'] this report. Good. How are you?

BUSINESSMAN  I think I'm putting on weight.

DIETICIAN  Oh? You're not managing to lose weight [literally 'slim']? Why not?

BUSINESSMAN  I'm always hungry. I'm always thirsty. What should I do?

DIETICIAN  Do your exercises regularly. Eat salad whenever you can. [Literally 'Seize every opportunity to eat salad.']

BUSINESSMAN  And what shouldn't I do?

DIETICIAN  Never choose cakes. Never choose ice cream. Never choose cheese.

BUSINESSMAN  Fine. And what about wine?

DIETICIAN  Never fill your glass completely.

BUSINESSMAN  Do you vouch for this diet (Madam)?

DIETICIAN  Yes. One thing's certain: if you put on weight, you shorten your life.

BUSINESSMAN  Yes (Madam). You're right.

# Week 4

- *the perfect tense (enabling you to talk about the past), in both its affirmative and negative forms*
- *possessive adjectives ('my', 'your', 'his', etc)*
- *the expression 'c'est' ('it is')*
- *expressing the time*
- *an important irregular verb, 'partir' ('to leave')*
- *more numbers*
- *seasons, months, dates, and days of the week*
- *the position of adjectives (before/after the noun)*

## 17 THE PERFECT TENSE

The French perfect tense translates all three forms of the English past: 'I have spoken', 'I did speak', or 'I spoke'. As in English, the perfect is usually (although not always) formed with **avoir** (to have) and a past participle, e.g. **j'ai parlé**.

To form the past participle in French we:

change the **-er** of the infinitive into **-é**

change the **-ir** of the infinitive into **-i**

| Verbs ending in **-er** | Verbs ending in **-ir** |
| --- | --- |
| **j'ai parlé** | **j'ai fini** |
| **tu as preparé** | **tu as garanti** |
| **il a habité** | **il a choisi** |
| **elle a travaillé** | **elle a grossi** |
| **nous avons regardé** | **nous avons maigri** |
| **vous avez écouté** | **vous avez saisi** |
| **ils ont voyagé** | **ils ont raccourci** |
| **elles ont téléphoné** | **elles ont rempli** |

### VOCABULARY

| | |
| --- | --- |
| **le document** | document |
| **l'Italie (f.)** | Italy |
| **la Manche** | Channel |

| | |
|---|---|
| **copier** | to copy |
| **dépenser** | to spend (money) |
| **passer** | to spend (time) |
| **traverser** | to cross |

## IMITATED PRONUNCIATION (17)

pahr-lay; pray-pah-ray; ah-bee-tay; etc., fee-nee;
gah-rah*ng*-tee; shwah-zee; etc.,do-kü-mah*ng*;
ee-tah-lee; mah*ng*sh; kop-yay; day-pah*ng*-say;
pah-say; trah-vairr-say.

## Exercise 16

Translate:

1 I have lived in France.
2 I have worked in Italy.
3 I have reserved the rooms.
4 She listened to the radio.
5 She watched the television.
6 She prepared the report.
7 He has put on weight.
8 He has chosen the cheese.
9 He has finished the book.
10 We copied the document.
11 We bought the car.
12 We telephoned.
13 You guaranteed the CD player.
14 You seized the opportunity.
15 You invited the President.
16 They (m.) have lost weight.
17 They (f.) have spent 15 euros.
18 They (f.) have crossed the Channel.

You will also wish to say what you have not done:

**je n'ai pas copié**
**tu n'as pas traversé**
**il n'a pas passé**
**elle n'a pas acheté**
**nous n'avons pas invité**
**vous n'avez pas garanti**
**ils n'ont pas rempli**
**elles n'ont pas fini**

Note the position of **pas** every time.

## Exercise 17

Answer the questions as follows:
Avez-vous travaillé en Italie?    Have you worked in Italy?
Non, je n'ai pas travaillé en Italie.    No, I haven't worked in Italy.

**1** Avez-vous réservé la chambre?
**2** Avez-vous écouté le CD?
**3** A-t-il regardé le film?
**4** A-t-elle préparé le document?
**5** Est-ce que nous avons fini?
**6** Est-ce qu'ils ont choisi?
**7** Est-ce qu'elles ont mangé?

## 19 POSSESSIVES: MY, YOURS, HIS, HERS, ETC

It is important to be able to establish ownership:

|              | m.sing. | f.sing. | m. & f. pl. |
|--------------|---------|---------|-------------|
| my           | **mon** | **ma**  | **mes**     |
| your (fam.)  | **ton** | **ta**  | **tes**     |
| his/her/its  | **son** | **sa**  | **ses**     |
| our          | **notre** | **notre** | **nos**  |
| your         | **votre** | **votre** | **vos**  |
| their        | **leur** | **leur** | **leurs**   |

Note that these adjectives agree with the thing possessed, not with the possessor:

| | |
|---|---|
| **ma femme**   | my wife            |
| **son mari**   | her husband        |
| **sa chambre** | his or her bedroom |
| **ses clés**   | his or her keys    |

However, note also that if the following noun begins with a vowel, the French use **mon, ton, son** instead of **ma, ta, sa**, even if the noun is feminine:

| | |
|---|---|
| **mon amie**    | my friend        |
| **ton agence**  | your agency      |
| **son enquête** | his/her survey   |

This sounds more pleasant to the French ear.

### VOCABULARY

| | |
|---|---|
| **le vol**                    | flight               |
| **l'horaire (m.)**            | timetable            |
| **la ceinture de sécurité**   | seat belt            |
| **la place**                  | seat                 |
| **attacher**                  | to fasten, to attach |
| **premier, première (f.)**    | first                |

## IMITATED PRONUNCIATION (19)

mo*ng*; mah; may; to*ng*; tah; tay; so*ng*; sah; say; notr;
noh; votr; voh; le*r*r; fahm; mah-ree; vol; o-rairr;
sa*ng*-tür de*r* say-kü-ree-tay; plahs; ah-tah-shay;
pre*r*m-yay; pre*r*m-yairr.

## Exercise 18

Translate:

1 Your first flight.
2 Fasten your seat belt.
3 Where are our tickets?
4 Here is her passport.
5 Here is his seat.
6 Their suitcases are in the plane.
7 Where are my newspapers?

## 20 THE EXPRESSION C'EST ('IT IS')

| | |
|---|---|
| **C'est facile.** | It is easy. |
| **C'est difficile.** | It is difficult. |
| **C'est très important.** | It is very important. |
| **C'est moins cher.** | It is less expensive. |

### VOCABULARY

| | |
|---|---|
| **possible** | possible |
| **impossible** | impossible |
| **magnifique** | wonderful |
| **affreux** | dreadful |
| **tôt** | early |
| **tard** | late |

## IMITATED PRONUNCIATION

say; mwah*ng*; po-seebl; a*ng*-po-seebl; mahn-yee-feek; ah-fre*r*; toh; tahr.

---

### Exercise 19 _____

Give the opposite of:

1 C'est intéressant.
2 C'est bon.
3 C'est possible.
4 C'est facile.
5 C'est magnifique.
6 C'est tard.

---

### 21  THE TIME

If you intend to keep appointments, catch trains and buses, and so on, you must be familiar with the way in which the French express the time:

**Quelle heure est-il?**  What time is it?
**Il est une heure.**  It is one o'clock.
**Il est deux heures.**  It is two o'clock.
**Il est trois heures.**  It is three o'clock.
**Il est quatre heures.**  It is four o'clock.
**Il est midi.**  It is midday.
**Il est minuit.**  It is midnight.

**Il est cinq heures et quart.**  It is a quarter past five.
**Il est cinq heures et demie.**  It is half past five.
**Il est six heures moins le quart.**  It is a quarter to six.

**Il est six heures dix.**  It is ten past six.
**Il est sept heures moins cinq.**  It is five to seven.

**À quelle heure?**  At what time?
**À huit heures.**  At eight o'clock.

**À neuf heures du matin.**
At nine in the morning.
**À neuf heures du soir.**
At nine in the evening.
**À deux heures de l'après-midi.**
At two in the afternoon.

## VOCABULARY

| | |
|---|---|
| **le car** | coach |
| **le bateau** | boat |
| **l'aéroglisseur (m.)** | hovercraft |
| **le président** | president, chairman |
| **la conférence de presse** | press conference |
| **arriver** | to arrive |

### IRREGULAR VERB

**partir** (to leave)

Present tense
**je pars**
**tu pars**
**il/elle part**
**nous partons**
**vous partez**
**ils/elles partent**

## IMITATED PRONUNCIATION (21)

kel e*rr* ay teel; eel ay ün e*rr*; eel ay der ze*rr*; trwah ze*rr*;
mee-dee; meen-wee; kahr; de*r*-mee; ah kel e*rr*; ah ne*r*
ve*rr* dü mah-ta*ng*; dü swahr; de*r* lah-pray-mee-dee;
kahr; bah-toh; ah-ay-roh-glee-se*rr*; pray-zee-dah*ng*;
ko*ng*-fay-rah*ng*ss der press; ah-ree-vay; pahr-teerr; pahr;
pahr-to*ng*; pahr-tay; pahrt.

## Exercise 20

Add 15 minutes to the time stated:

**1** Il est deux heures.

**2** Il est quatre heures et quart.

**3** Il est six heures moins le quart.

**4** Il est huit heures cinq.

**5** Le train arrive à dix heures.

**6** Le car arrive à onze heures et demie.

**7** Le bateau part à midi dix.

**8** L'aéroglisseur part à minuit et demi*.

**9** Le Président arrive à neuf heures.

**10** La conférence de presse est à dix heures.

*'Demi' agrees with 'minuit' (m.); write 'demie' to agree with 'heure' (f.).

## 22 MORE NUMBERS

Here are some more numbers:

| | | | |
|---|---|---|---|
| 16 | seize | 33 | trente-trois |
| 17 | dix-sept | 40 | quarante |
| 18 | dix-huit | 41 | quarante et un |
| 19 | dix-neuf | 42 | quarante-deux |
| 20 | vingt | 50 | cinquante |
| 21 | vingt et un | 51 | cinquante et un |
| 22 | vingt-deux | 52 | cinquante-deux |
| 23 | vingt-trois | 60 | soixante |
| 30 | trente | 61 | soixante et un |
| 31 | trente et un | 62 | soixante-deux |
| 32 | trente-deux | | |

### IMITATED PRONUNCIATION (22)

sez; dee-set; deez-weet; deez-nerf; va*ng*; va*ng*-tay-u*ng*; va*ng*t-der; va*ng*t-trwah; trah*ng*t; kah-rah*ng*t; sa*ng*-kah*ng*t; swah-sah*ng*t.

## 23 SEASONS OF THE YEAR

| | |
|---|---|
| **le printemps** | spring |
| **l'été (m.)** | summer |
| **l'automne (m.)** | autumn |
| **l'hiver (m.)** | winter |

The seasons are all masculine.

| | |
|---|---|
| **en été** | in summer |
| **en automne** | in autumn |
| **en hiver** | in winter |
| but | |
| **au printemps** | in spring |

## 24 MONTHS OF THE YEAR

| | |
|---|---|
| **janvier** | January |
| **février** | February |
| **mars** | March |
| **avril** | April |
| **mai** | May |
| **juin** | June |
| **juillet** | July |
| **août** | August |
| **septembre** | September |
| **octobre** | October |
| **novembre** | November |
| **décembre** | December |

Note that the months of the year are not written with a capital letter in French.

### IMITATED PRONUNCIATION (23/24)

ler pra*ng*-tah*ng*; lay-tay; loh-ton; lee-vairr; zhah*ng*v-yay; fayvr-yay; mahrss; ah-vreel; may; zhwa*ng*; zhwee-yay; oo OR oot; sep-tah*ng*br; ok-tobr; no-vah*ng*br; day-sah*ng*br.

## 25  DATES

**Quelle date sommes-nous aujourd'hui?**
What is the date today?
**Nous sommes le deux janvier.**
It's the 2nd of January.
**Nous sommes le huit février.**
It's the 8th of February.
**Nous sommes le quinze mars.**
It's the 15th of March.
**Nous sommes le vingt avril.**
It's the 20th of April.
**Nous sommes le trente mai.**
It's the 30th of May.

Note for the 'first' of each month we use **le premier**:

**le premier juin**  the 1st of June
**le premier juillet**  the 1st of July
*but*
**le vingt et un août**  the 21st of August
**le trente et un octobre**  the 31st of October

Note also how you say 'in' a certain month:

**en août**  in August
**en septembre**  in September
**en octobre**  in October
**en novembre**  in November

4

## Exercise 21

Write in full the following dates:

1 New Year's Day
2 May Day
3 the storming of the Bastille
4 Christmas Day
5 Armistice Day
6 The first day of Spring

## 4 26 DAYS OF THE WEEK

| | |
|---|---|
| **lundi** | Monday |
| **mardi** | Tuesday |
| **mercredi** | Wednesday |
| **jeudi** | Thursday |
| **vendredi** | Friday |
| **samedi** | Saturday |
| **dimanche** | Sunday |

Note that the days of the week are not written with a capital letter in French.

**Avez-vous travaillé lundi?**
Did you work on Monday?
**Pierre téléphone jeudi.**
Pierre is telephoning on Thursday.
**Pierre téléphone le jeudi.**
Pierre telephones on Thursdays.

Note that the preposition 'on' is omitted in French. **Le** indicates that the action takes place regularly.

## IMITATED PRONUNCIATION (25/26)

daht; oh-zhoor-dwee; lung-dee; mahr-dee;
mairr-krer-dee; zher-dee; vahng-drer-dee;
sahm-dee; dee-mahngsh.

## Exercise 22

Translate:

1 I worked on Monday.
2 I listened to the radio on Tuesday.
3 I watched television on Wednesday.
4 I finished the report on Thursday.
5 I bought a book on Friday.
6 I telephoned my wife on Saturday.
7 I spoke Spanish on Sunday.
8 I work on Mondays.
9 She listens to the radio on Tuesdays.
10 We watch television on Wednesdays.

4

## 27 THE POSITION OF ADJECTIVES

In French adjectives are usually placed after the noun:

**un livre difficile**  a difficult book
**un médecin français**  a French doctor
**une voiture américaine**  an American car
**une langue importante**  an important language

The following adjectives normally precede the noun:

| | |
|---|---|
| **bon, bonne (f.)** | good |
| **mauvais** | bad |
| **petit** | small |
| **grand** | large |
| **joli** | pretty |
| **jeune** | young |
| **vieux (m. sing. & pl.)** | old |
|   **vieil (m. sing.** before a vowel or h**)** | |
|   **vieille (f.)** | |
|   **vieilles (f. pl.)** | |
| **nouveau (m. sing.)** | new |
|   **nouvel (m. sing** before a vowel or h**)** | |
|   **nouvelle (f.)** | |
|   **nouveaux (m. pl.)** | |
|   **nouvelles (f. pl.)** | |

Examples:
**un bon employé**  a good employee
**un jeune pilote**  a young pilot
**un vieil ordinateur**  an old computer
**un nouvel appareil-photo**  a new camera
**une mauvaise cliente**  a bad client
**une jolie secrétaire**  a pretty secretary

## IMITATED PRONUNCIATION (27)

zho-lee; zhern; vyer; vyay'ee; noo-voh; noo-vel;
ahng-plwah-yay; klee-yahngt; ser-kray-tairr.

| | |
|---|---|
| **Londres (m.)** | London |
| **l'argent (m.)** | money |
| **le départ** | departure |
| **la conversation** | conversation |
| **la semaine** | week |
| **les vacances (f.)** | holidays |
| **la nourriture** | food |
| **la chaleur** | heat |
| **visiter** | to visit |
| **trouver** | to find |
| **consulter** | to consult |
| **il faut** | one must |
| **indigeste** | indigestible |
| **insupportable** | unbearable |
| **moi** | me (see section 54) |
| **un peu** | a little |
| **à l'avance** | in advance |
| **des (de + les = des)** | of the |
| **d'accord** | O.K., fine |
| **le retour** | return |

4

## IMITATED PRONUNCIATION

longdr; ahr-zhahng; day-pahr; kong-vairr-sah-see-ong;
ser-men; vah-kahngss; noo-ree-türr; shah-lerr;
vee-zee-tay; troo-vay; kong-sül-tay; eel foh;
ang-dee-zhest; ang-sü-porr-tahbl; mwah; ung per;
ah lah-vahngss; day.

*À une agence de voyages à Londres*

Une conversation entre un employé français et une cliente américaine qui habite à Londres. La cliente saisit l'occasion pour parler français.

**4**

CLIENTE **Mon mari et moi, nous désirons passer deux semaines en France au printemps. Nous avons visité l'Italie en août, mais nous n'avons pas passé de bonnes vacances.**

EMPLOYÉ **Ah? Pourquoi pas?**

CLIENTE **Nous avons trouvé la nourriture un peu indigeste, nous avons trouvé la chaleur insupportable, et nous avons dépensé beaucoup d'argent.**

EMPLOYÉ **Avez-vous l'intention de voyager en avion?**

CLIENTE **Non, par le train, c'est plus agréable.**

EMPLOYÉ **Un petit instant, Madame, je consulte l'horaire de l'Eurostar. Il y a un départ à huit heures, à neuf heures, à dix heures, à onze heures, etc. Il faut réserver les places à l'avance.**

CLIENTE **Oui, d'accord. Départ 9 avril, retour 23 avril.**

EMPLOYÉ **Un instant, s'il vous plaît.**

*At a travel agency in London*

A conversation between a French clerk and an American client who lives in London. The client seizes the opportunity to speak French.

CLIENT  My husband and I want to spend two weeks in France in the spring. We visited Italy in August, but we didn't have a good holiday.

CLERK  Oh? Why not?

CLIENT  We found the food a little heavy [literally 'indigestible'], we found the heat unbearable, and we spent a lot of money.

CLERK  Do you intend to travel by plane?

CLIENT  No, by train, it's more pleasant.

CLERK  Just one moment, Madam. I'll consult the Eurostar timetable. There's a departure at eight o'clock, at nine o'clock, at ten o'clock, at eleven o'clock, etc. One must reserve seats in advance.

CLIENT  Yes, O.K. Departure 9 April, return 23 April.

CLERK  One moment, please.

**4**

## Self-assessment test 1  A–C

This self-assessment test, based on weeks 1–4, will enable you to check on your progress and to see whether any revision is needed. Deduct one mark for every grammatical mistake or wrong spelling. The answers and score assessment are in the Key.

**A** Nouns    Total: 8 marks
Give the French for:

1 the doctor          5 my car
2 the computer        6 my keys
3 some wine           7 this train
4 some beer           8 these newspapers

**B** Adjectives    Total: 5 marks
Give the opposite of:

1 pauvre              4 magnifique
2 malheureux          5 facile
3 intéressant

**C** Verbs    Total: 10 marks
Which French verb do you associate with the following?

1 la télévision
2 la radio
3 la méthode Hugo
4 un sport
5 la ceinture de sécurité
6 une chambre d'hôtel
7 une agence de voyages
8 l'occasion pour parler français
9 l'horaire des trains
10 la Manche

**D** The time    Total: 8 marks
Add fifteen minutes to the time mentioned:

1  Le train part à six heures.
2  Le car part à huit heures et demie.
3  Le Président arrive à dix heures cinq.
4  La conférence de presse est à onze heures et demie.

**E** Days of the week    Total: 4 marks
Write down the day before the one shown:

**1** jeudi      **3** samedi
**2** lundi      **4** mercredi

**F** Total: 4 marks
What difference in meaning is there between 'jeudi' and 'le jeudi'?

**G** Months of the year    Total: 4 marks
Write down the date a month after the one shown:

**1** le deux janvier
**2** le cinq mars
**3** le douze mai
**4** le trente et un juillet

**H** The perfect tense    Total: 8 marks
It all happened on Monday! Answer these questions in the perfect past, as in this example:
Q- Avez-vous l'intention de regarder le film?
A- Non, j'ai regardé le film lundi.

**1** Avez-vous l'intention de réserver les chambres?
**2** A-t-il l'intention de finir le livre?
**3** A-t-elle l'intention de copier le document?
**4** Ont-ils l'intention de téléphoner?

**I** The perfect tense (negative)    Total: 16 marks
Give the French for:

**1** I haven't finished the report.
**2** She didn't telephone her husband on Saturday.
**3** We haven't visited Italy.
**4** They (m.) haven't lost weight.

**J** Numerals    Total: 18 marks
Complete the following, writing the totals in words:

**a)** 14 + 15            **f)** 30 + 20
**b)** 20 + 16            **g)** 10 + 5
**c)** 23 + 22            **h)** 30 + 32
**d)** 27 + 4             **i)** 14 + 2
**e)** 14 + 30

**K** Do you remember …?    Total: 1 mark
Which verb do the French use when talking about a person's age?

**L** Conversation (role-play)    Total: 14 marks
Play the part of the customer in this short scene:

CLIENTE  We want to spend two weeks in France in the spring. We visited Italy in August, but we found the heat unbearable.
EMPLOYÉ  Avez-vous l'intention de voyager en avion?
CLIENTE  No, by train, it's more pleasant.
EMPLOYÉ  Un petit instant, Madame, je consulte l'horaire de l'Eurostar. Il faut réserver les places à l'avance.
CLIENTE  Yes, O.K.! Departure 9 April, return 23 April.

# Week 5

- *regular and irregular '-re' verbs, in both present and perfect tenses*
- *introduction to adverbs*
- *the pronoun 'it'*
- *object pronouns (me, him, her, to him, to her, etc)*
- *using object pronouns with the perfect tense*
- *more irregular verbs, including the perfect tenses of 'être' and 'avoir'*

## 28  REGULAR VERBS ENDING IN -RE

A number of important verbs end in **-re**:

| | |
|---|---|
| **vendre** | to sell |
| **rendre** | to give back |
| **attendre** | to wait (for) |
| **entendre** | to hear |
| **descendre** | to take/bring down |
| **répondre** | to reply |
| **perdre** | to lose |

We form the present tense by removing the **-re** from the infinitive and adding:

| | | | |
|---|---|---|---|
| **je** | **-s** | **nous** | **-ons** |
| **tu** | **-s** | **vous** | **-ez** |
| **il/elle** | **-d** | **ils/elles** | **-ent** |

| | |
|---|---|
| **je vends** | **nous vendons** |
| **tu vends** | **vous vendez** |
| **il/elle vend** | **ils/elles vendent** |

The perfect tense is formed by changing the **-re** of the infinitive into **-u**:

| | |
|---|---|
| **j'ai vendu** | **nous avons vendu** |
| **tu as vendu** | **vous avez vendu** |
| **il/elle a vendu** | **ils/elles ont vendu** |

## VOCABULARY

| | |
|---|---|
| **les parents (m.)** | parents |
| **le frère** | brother |
| **la musique** | music |
| **la maison** | house |
| **la mère** | mother |
| **cela** | that |
| **dépendre de** | to depend on |
| **défendre** | to defend, to forbid |

## IMITATED PRONUNCIATION (28)

vah*ng*dr; rah*ng*dr; ah-tah*ng*dr; ah*ng*-tah*ng*dr;
day-sah*ng*dr; ray-po*ng*dr; pairrdr; vah*ng*; vah*ng*-do*ng*;
vah*ng*-day; vah*ng*d; vah*ng*-dü; pah-rah*ng*; frairr;
mü-zeek; may-zo*ng*; mairr; ser-lah; day-pah*ng*dr der;
day-fah*ng*dr.

## __Exercise 23__

Translate:

1  I am selling my car.
2  He is waiting for his wife.
3  We give back 60 euros.
4  That depends on my parents.
5  Do they (f.) hear the music?
6  She has sold her house.
7  We have not replied.
8  Have you brought down the luggage?
9  Are you (fam. sing.) waiting for your brother?
10  Have you (fam. sing.) lost your mother?

IRREGULAR VERBS ENDING IN -RE

The following **-re** verbs are irregular, taking a slightly different pattern in the present tense and a very different pattern in the perfect tense:

| | | | |
|---|---|---|---|
| **prendre** | to take | **comprendre** | to understand |
| **apprendre** | to learn | **surprendre** | to surprise |

Present
**je prends**          I take (or I am taking)
**tu prends**
**il/elle prend**
**nous prenons**
**vous prenez**
**ils/elles prennent**

Perfect
**j'ai pris**          I took (or I have taken)
**j'ai appris**        I learnt
**j'ai compris**       I understood
**j'ai surpris**       I surprised

## IMITATED PRONUNCIATION (29)

prahngdr; ah-prah*ng*dr; ko*ng*-prah*ng*dr; sür-prah*ng*dr; prah*ng*; prer-no*ng*; prer-nay; pren; pree; ah-pree; ko*ng*-pree; sür-pree.

## Exercise 24

Change the present to the past and vice versa:

1 Est-ce que vous prenez le train?
2 J'apprends le français.
3 Avez-vous appris la langue?
4 Avez-vous compris?
5 Tu surprends souvent ton professeur?

The following irregular **-re** verbs have a similar pattern to that of the '**prendre**' group but the consonant is doubled in the **nous**, **vous**, and **ils/elles** forms:

| | |
|---|---|
| **mettre** | to put |
| **permettre** | to permit |
| **promettre** | to promise |
| **soumettre** | to submit |

Present
| | |
|---|---|
| **je mets** | I put (or I am putting) |
| **tu mets** | |
| **il/elle met** | |
| **nous mettons** | |
| **vous mettez** | |
| **ils/elles mettent** | |

Perfect
| | |
|---|---|
| **vous avez mis** | you put (or you have put) |
| **vous avez permis** | you permitted |
| **vous avez promis** | you have promised |
| **vous avez soumis** | you have submitted |

### VOCABULARY

| | |
|---|---|
| **le matin** | morning |
| **le dictionnaire** | dictionary |
| **le projet** | project, plan |
| **l'enfant (m. & f.)** | child |
| **l'annonce (f.)** | advertisement |
| **la lettre** | letter |
| **permettre de** | to allow to |
| **promettre de** | to promise to |
| **rentrer** | to return |
| **tôt** | early |
| **tard** | late |
| **déjà** | already |

Note the construction with **défendre** and **permettre**:

**Je défends à Paul de parler.**  I forbid Paul to speak.
**Je permets à Paul de parler.**  I allow Paul to speak.

## IMITATED PRONUNCIATION (30)

metr; pairr-metr; pro-metr; soo-metr; may; met-*ong*;
met-ay; met; mee; pairr-mee; pro-mee; soo-mee;
mah-ta*ng*; deeks-yo-nairr; pro-zhay; ah*ng*-fah*ng*;
ah-no*ng*s; letr; rah*ng*-tray; toh; tahr; day-zhah.

### Exercise 25

Change the present to the past and vice versa:

1 Je mets une annonce dans le journal.
2 Il permet à sa secrétaire de partir tôt.
3 Vous promettez de répondre à la lettre?
4 Elle soumet le rapport ce matin.
5 Avez-vous mis le dictionnaire dans la valise?
6 Ont-ils permis à leurs enfants de rentrer tard?
7 Nous avons promis de parler français.
8 Avez-vous déjà soumis le projet?

**5**

## 31 ADVERBS: SAYING HOW THINGS ARE DONE

We often need to describe how things are done, for
example: rapidly, admirably, carefully.

In French, adverbs are formed by adding **-ment** to the
adjective, which is the equivalent of -ly in English:

**rapide** (rapid) becomes **rapidement** (rapidly)
**admirable** becomes **admirablement**
**rare** becomes **rarement**

If the adjective ends in a consonant, e.g. **malheureux**
(unfortunate), **-ment** is added to the feminine:

| | | |
|---|---|---|
| **immédiat** | **immédiate (f.)** | **immédiatement** |
| **général** | **générale (f.)** | **généralement** |
| **malheureux** | **malheureuse (f.)** | **malheureusement** |

## VOCABULARY

| | |
|---|---|
| **attentif, attentive (f.)** | careful |
| **complet, complète (f.)** | complete |
| **lent** | slow |
| **normal** | normal |
| **principal** | main |
| **temporaire** | temporary |

## IMITATED PRONUNCIATION (31)

rah-peed; rah-peed-mah*ng*; ahd-mee-rahbl;
ahd-mee-rah-bler-mah*ng*; rahr; rahr-mahng;
ee-mayd-yaht-mah*ng*; zhay-nay-rahl-mah*ng*;
mah-ler-rerz-mah*ng*; ah-tah*ng*-teef; ah-tah*ng*-teev;
ko*ng*-play; ko*ng*-plet; lah*ng*; norr-mahl; pra*ng*-see-pahl;
tah*ng*-po-rairr.

## ___ Exercise 26 ___

Form adverbs from the following adjectives:

1 rapide
2 facile
3 final
4 heureux
5 attentif
6 lent
7 complet
8 normal
9 principal
10 temporaire

When 'it' refers to something which has just been mentioned, we use the same word in French as for 'he' or 'she', depending on the gender of the noun:

**Le vin? Il est très bon.**  The wine? It's very good.
**La voiture? Elle est chère.**  The car? It's expensive.

Referring to things, 'they' is expressed by **ils** or **elles**:

**Les trains? Ils sont rapides.**
The trains? They're fast.
**Les places? Elles sont réservées.**
The seats? They're reserved.

5

## VOCABULARY

| | |
|---|---|
| **l'appareil (m.)** | machine |
| **le restaurant** | restaurant |
| **le produit** | product |
| **le message** | message |
| **le répondeur** | telephone |
| **automatique** | answering machine |
| **la poche** | pocket |
| **la qualité** | quality |
| **l'explication (f.)** | explanation |
| **clair** | clear |
| **en anglais** | in English |
| **excellent** | excellent |

## IMITATED PRONUNCIATION

ah-pah-ray'ee; res-to-rah*ng*; pro-dwee; may-sahzh;
ray-po*ng*-de*rr*; oh-toh-mah-teek; posh; kah-lee-tay;
eks-plee-kah-see-o*ng*; klairr; ah*ng* nah*ng*-glay;
ek-sel-ah*ng*.

## Exercise 27

Translate:

1 The report? It's very important.
2 The beer? It's bad.
3 The pocket? It's full.
4 The machine? It's excellent.
5 The restaurant? It's closed.
6 The quality? It's very good.
7 The products? They're French.
8 The messages? They're in English.
9 The explanation? It's not clear.
10 The answering machine? It's not expensive.

## 33 OBJECT PRONOUNS: ME, HIM, HER, TO HIM, TO HER, IT, ETC

Study the following:

**Michel le rencontre** Michel meets him
**Michel la rencontre** Michel meets her
**Michel les rencontre** Michel meets them
**Hélène le vend (masc. word)** Hélène sells it
**Hélène la vend (fem. word)** Hélène sells it
**Paul nous félicite** Paul congratulates us
**Paul vous félicite** Paul congratulates you
**Sophie me choisit** Sophie chooses me
**Sophie te choisit** Sophie chooses you
**Sophie vous comprend** Sophie understands you

You will have noticed that:

'me', 'him', 'her', 'us', 'them', etc come before the verb;

the words for 'him', 'her', 'it', and 'them' are just like the words for 'the';

the words for 'us' and 'you' are just like those for 'we' and 'you' (subject);

'me' in French is **me**; 'you', familiar singular, is **te**; 'you', familiar plural, remains **vous**.

**Me, nous, vous,** and **te** can also mean 'to me', 'to us', 'to you':

**il me parle**  he speaks to me
**il nous répète**  he repeats to us
**elle vous répond**  she replies to you
**elle te vend**  she sells to you (fam.)

Both 'to him' and 'to her' are translated by **lui**:

**je lui répète**  I repeat to him (or to her)

We express 'to them' by **leur**:

**je leur parle**  I speak to them

Sometimes the 'to' is not expressed in English, although clearly intended. Compare the French and the English:

**Je lui vends la voiture.**  I sell him the car.
**Nous leur téléphonons.**  We telephone them.

NOTE: **me, le, la,** and **te** become **m', l', t'** in front of a vowel or h: **il m'invite; elle l'écoute; je t'invite**

## VOCABULARY

| | |
|---|---|
| **le client** | client |
| **le mode d'emploi** | operating instructions |
| **l'ami (m.)** | friend |
| **l'amie (f.)** | friend |
| **la leçon** | lesson |
| **la commerçante** | shopkeeper |
| **brancher** | to plug in |
| **mettre en marche** | to start, to set going |

## IMITATED PRONUNCIATION

klee-yah*ng*; mod dah*ng*-plwah; ah-mee; ah-mee;
le*r*-so*ng*; ko-mairr-sah*ng*t; brahng-shay;
metr ah*ng* mahrsh.

## Exercise 28

Answer the questions using pronouns, as follows:
Vous me comprenez? Do you understand me?
Oui, je vous comprends. Yes, I understand you.

1 Elle me cherche?
2 Elle vous consulte?
3 Vous rencontrez le client?
4 Vous copiez la leçon?
5 Il invite Nicole?
6 Il exporte les voitures?
7 Comprenons-nous le mode d'emploi?
8 Branchons-nous la radio?
9 Mettons-nous l'appareil en marche?
10 Copions-nous le document?
11 Elles nous répondent en français?
12 Ils téléphonent à Pierre?
13 Ils téléphonent à Nicole?
14 Ils téléphonent à Pierre et à Nicole?
15 Vous parlez à la commerçante?
16 Vous répondez à vos amis?
17 Vous défendez à vos enfants de rentrer tard?

When you use a direct object pronoun with the perfect tense, the past participle of the verb has to agree in gender and number with the pronoun:

| | |
|---|---|
| **je l'ai invité** | I invited him |
| **je l'ai invitée** | I invited her |
| **je les ai invités** | I invited them (men or men and women) |
| **je les ai invitées** | I invited them (women) |
| | |
| **vous l'avez copié** | you copied it **(le document)** |
| **vous l'avez copiée** | you copied it **(la leçon)** |
| **vous les avez copiés** | you copied them **(les documents)** |
| **vous les avez copiées** | you copied them **(les leçons)** |
| **vous les avez copiés** | you copied them **(les documents et les leçons)** |
| | |
| **il m'a trouvé** | he found me (man speaking) |
| **il m'a trouvée** | he found me (woman speaking) |
| **il nous a trouvés** | he found us (men speaking) |
| **il nous a trouvées** | he found us (women speaking) |
| **il nous a trouvés** | he found us (men and women speaking) |
| | |
| **elle vous a consulté** | she consulted you (m. doctor) |
| **elle vous a consultée** | she consulted you (f. doctor) |
| **elle vous a consultés** | she consulted you (m. doctors) |
| **elle vous a consultées** | she consulted you (f. doctors) |
| **elle vous a consultés** | she consulted you (m./f. doctors) |

Note that this does NOT apply when the pronoun is the indirect object, meaning 'to me', 'to him', etc.

5

The pronunciation of all these endings is the same, i.e. 'ay'. However, when the past participle ends in a consonant, for example **compris**, the addition of the feminine ending '**e**' or '**es**' results in this consonant being sounded:

**je l'ai comprise**   I understood her
zher lay ko*ng*-preez

**je les ai apprises** I learnt them (**les leçons**, for example)
zher lay zay ah-preez

## Exercise 29

Answer the questions as follows:

Avez-vous rencontré le client? Did you meet the client?
Oui, je l'ai rencontré. Yes, I met him.

1  Avez-vous invité Pierre?
2  Avez-vous invité Nicole?
3  Avez-vous invité Pierre et Nicole?
4  A-t-il exporté les voitures?
5  A-t-elle consulté le médecin?
6  A-t-elle consulté la diététicienne?
7  A-t-elle consulté le médecin et la diététicienne?
8  Ont-ils branché la radio?
9  Ont-ils réservé les chambres?
10 Ont-ils perdu la clé?
11 Avons-nous compris le mode d'emploi?
12 Avons-nous compris la leçon?
13 Avons-nous compris les leçons?
14 Avons-nous compris les livres?
15 Avez-vous mis le CD dans votre poche?

### VOCABULARY

| | |
|---|---|
| l'appel téléphonique (m.) | telephone call |
| ici | here |
| tout | everything |
| même | even |
| depuis | since |
| peut-être | perhaps |
| il y a | ago |
| seul | single, only |
| utiliser | to use |
| aux (à + les = aux) | to the |
| répéter | to repeat |

(See section 81 for how **répéter** slightly changes its spelling in the present tense.)

## IRREGULAR VERBS

**lire** (to read)

Present tense
| | |
|---|---|
| **je lis** | **nous lisons** |
| **tu lis** | **vous lisez** |
| **il/elle lit** | **ils/elles lisent** |

Perfect tense
**j'ai lu**, etc

**faire** (to do, to make)

Present tense
| | |
|---|---|
| **je fais** | **nous faisons** |
| **tu fais** | **vous faites** |
| **il/elle fait** | **ils/elles font** |

Perfect tense
**j'ai fait, etc**

| **être** (to be) | **avoir** (to have) |
|---|---|
| Perfect tense | Perfect tense |
| **j'ai été**, etc | **j'ai eu**, etc |

## IMITATED PRONUNCIATION

ah-pel tay-lay-fo-neek; ee-see; too; mem; der-pwee; per-tetr; eel yah; serl; ü-tee-lee-zay; oh; ray-pay-tay; zher ray-pet; tü ray-pet; eel ray-pet; noo ray-pay-tong; voo ray-pay-tay; eel ray-pet; leerr; zher lee; tü lee; eel lee; noo lee-zong; voo lee-zay; eel leez; zhay lü; fairr; zher fay; tü fay; eel fay; noo fer-zong; voo fet; eel fong; zhay fay; etr; zhay ay-tay; ah-vwahr; zhay ü.

## CONVERSATION

*Une conversation entre une commerçante et un client*

CLIENT **Bonjour, Madame. Il y a deux semaines vous m'avez vendu un répondeur automatique. Malheureusement, il ne répond pas aux appels téléphoniques de mes amis.**

COMMERÇANTE **Je suis surprise d'apprendre cela, Monsieur. Nos répondeurs sont d'excellente qualité. Avez-vous lu le mode d'emploi?**

CLIENT **Oui, je l'ai lu très attentivement. Attendez, je l'ai ici dans ma poche. Mais, où est-il? Je l'ai peut-être perdu.**

COMMERÇANTE **Ce n'est pas grave, Monsieur. Avez-vous branché l'appareil correctement? Avez-vous mis l'appareil en marche? Avez-vous compris les explications?**

CLIENT **Oui, j'ai tout compris et j'ai tout fait correctement. J'ai même défendu à mes enfants de l'utiliser.**

COMMERÇANTE **Permettez-moi de vous répéter, Monsieur, que nos produits sont d'excellente qualité. Si vous n'avez pas eu un seul message depuis deux semaines, la seule explication possible, c'est que personne ne vous téléphone!**

5

*A conversation between a shopkeeper and a customer*

CUSTOMER  Good morning. Two weeks ago you sold me an answering machine. Unfortunately, it doesn't answer my friends' telephone calls.

SHOPKEEPER  I'm surprised to hear [learn] that, Sir. Our answering machines are of excellent quality. Have you read the instruction booklet?

CUSTOMER  Yes, I read it very carefully. One moment [wait], I have it here in my pocket. But, where is it? Perhaps I've lost it.

SHOPKEEPER  It doesn't matter, Sir. Did you plug the machine in correctly? Did you start the machine? Did you understand the instructions [explanations]?

CUSTOMER  Yes, I understood everything and I did everything correctly. I've even forbidden my children to use it.

SHOPKEEPER  Allow me to repeat, Sir, that our products are of excellent quality. If you haven't had a single message for two weeks, the only possible explanation is that no-one telephones you!

5

# Week 6

- prepositions: in, to, from, etc
- the expression 'il y a' ('there is/are')
- the comparative and superlative of adjectives and adverbs, and irregular forms ('good/better/best')
- talking about the weather
- verbs that form their past tense with 'être'
- the expressions 'je voudrais' and 'il faut' ('I would like ...', 'one must/has to')

## 35 PREPOSITIONS: IN, TO, FROM, ETC

Here are some useful French prepositions. Many of them are used to indicate position:

| | |
|---|---|
| **dans** | in |
| **en** | in/to |
| **sur** | on |
| **sous** | under |
| **devant** | in front of |
| **derrière** | behind |
| **près de** | near |
| **à côté de** | next to |
| **en face de** | opposite |
| **à** | at/to |
| **de** | of/from |
| **pour** | for |
| **avec** | with |
| **sans** | without |
| **après** | after |
| **avant** | before |

We saw in previous chapters that the French do not say 'à le' or 'à les' but **au** and **aux**; instead of 'de le' and 'de les', they say **du** and **des**.

Examples:

| | |
|---|---|
| **au musée** | at/to the museum |
| **à la boulangerie** | at/to the baker's |
| **aux magasins** | at/to the shops |
| **du bureau de poste** | of/from the post office |

| | |
|---|---|
| **de la pharmacie** | of/from the chemist's |
| **des hôtels** | of/from the hotels |
| **dans la voiture** | in the car |
| **en France** | in/to France |
| **à côté de la boucherie** | next to the butcher's |
| **en face de la poissonnerie** | opposite the fishmonger's |
| **près de l'épicerie** | near the food store |
| **sur la table** | on the table |
| **sous la chaise** | under the chair |
| **devant l'hôpital** | in front of the hospital |
| **derrière l'université** | behind the university |
| **avec mon mari** | with my husband |
| **sans difficulté** | without difficulty |
| **après le petit déjeuner** | after breakfast |
| **avant le dîner** | before dinner |

NOTE: Both **dans** and **en** mean 'in', but **dans** is more specific, i.e. **dans** is generally used before **le**, **la**, **les**, **un**, **une**, **mon**, **votre**, etc; otherwise **en** is used. Contrast:

| | |
|---|---|
| **dans la voiture de mon frère** | in my brother's car |
| **en voiture** | by (in) car |
| **dans le sud de la France** | in the south of France |
| **en France** | in France |

Note also the following difference:

**dans deux semaines**  in two weeks' time
(I'll begin the work **'dans deux semaines'**)

**en deux semaines** within two weeks
(I did the work **'en deux semaines'**)

## 36 'IL Y A' ('THERE IS/ARE')

We have already met **il y a**, but let us look at this very useful expression more closely. It means 'there is' or 'there are' and can, therefore, be used with both singular and plural nouns:

**Il y a un taxi devant l'hôtel.**
There's a taxi in front of the hotel.
**Il y a des journaux ici.**
There are some newspapers here.
**Est-ce qu'il y a une banque ici?**
Is there a bank here?

### VOCABULARY

| | |
|---|---|
| **le restaurant** | restaurant |
| **le supermarché** | supermarket |
| **le tunnel** | tunnel |
| **le numéro de téléphone** | telephone number |
| **le cinéma** | cinema |
| **le théâtre** | theatre |
| **le spectacle** | show |
| **l'ami (m.)** | friend |
| **les États-Unis** | United States |
| **la serviette** | briefcase, towel, napkin |
| **l'église (f.)** | church |
| **la librairie** | bookshop |
| **la bibliothèque** | library |
| **la cabine téléphonique** | telephone booth |
| **l'amie (f.)** | friend |
| **c'est difficile de** | it is difficult to |
| **Angleterre** | England |

6

## IRREGULAR VERBS

**aller** (to go)

Present tense
**je vais**
**tu vas**
**il/elle va**
**nous allons**
**vous allez**
**ils/elles vont**

**venir** (to come)

Present tense
**je viens**
**tu viens**
**il/elle vient**
**nous venons vous venez**
**ils/elles viennent**

## IMITATED PRONUNCIATION

We feel that you should now be fairly confident as far as the pronunciation is concerned and we are discontinuing the imitated pronunciation at this point. You are advised, of course, to continue using the CDs in conjunction with this book to perfect your pronunciation or consider purchasing them if you haven't already.

## Exercise 30

Translate:

1 There's a briefcase on the table.
2 There's a taxi in front of the hotel.
3 There's a restaurant behind the church.
4 There's a supermarket next to the bank.
5 There's a bookshop opposite the university.
6 Is there a telephone booth near the station?
7 Are there any English books in the library?
8 Is there a tunnel under the Channel?
9 I'm going to the cinema.
10 She's going to the United States.
11 Do you have the telephone number of the theatre?
12 I have bought a newspaper for my friend.
13 She's learning French with some CDs.
14 It's difficult to work without my secretary.
15 Let's eat after the show.
16 Let's telephone before 9 o'clock.

**6**

## 37 COMPARISON OF ADJECTIVES

In English we make comparisons by adding 'er' to the adjective or by using 'more' or 'less'; in French we simply put **plus** (more) and **moins** (less) in front of the adjective:

**Cet hôtel est grand.**
This hotel is large.
**Cet hôtel est plus grand.**
This hotel is larger.
**Cette lettre est importante.**
This letter is important.
**Cette lettre est plus importante.**
This letter is more important.
**Ce livre est moins difficile.**
This book is less difficult.

We express 'than' by **que**:

**La cathédrale est plus belle que l'église.**
The cathedral is more beautiful than the church.
**Le film est moins intéressant que le livre.**
The film is less interesting than the book.

Note also:

**aussi ... que**    as ... as
**pas si ... que**    not so ... as

**L'aéroglisseur est aussi rapide que le tunnel sous la Manche.**
The hovercraft is as fast as the Channel tunnel.
**Le train n'est pas si rapide que l'avion.**
The train is not as fast as the plane.

## 38 COMPARISON OF ADVERBS

Adverbs follow the same pattern as adjectives:

**Pierre travaille lentement.**
Pierre works slowly.
**Paul travaille plus lentement que Pierre.**
Paul works more slowly than Pierre.

| | |
|---|---|
| **le banquier** | banker |
| **le facteur** | postman |
| **le russe** | Russian language |
| **l'actrice** | actress |
| **courageux** | brave |
| **distinct** | distinct |
| **beau (m.)** | beautiful |
|   **bel (m.** before a vowel or h) | |
|   **beaux (m. pl.)** | |
|   **belle (f.)** | |
|   **belles (f. pl.)** | |

## Exercise 31

Translate:

1  The banker is richer than the teacher.
2  The postman is poorer than the lawyer.
3  The pilot is as brave as the astronaut.
4  French is not so difficult as Russian
   (say *the* French … *the* Russian).
5  She speaks more distinctly than Paul.
6  He listens more attentively than his brother.

6

NOTE We have seen that 'than' is translated by **que**. However, when 'than' is followed by a number, we use **de** in place of **que**:

**J'ai plus de 40 euros.** I have more than 40 euros.

## 39 SUPERLATIVE OF ADJECTIVES

In English, we form the superlative by adding '-est' to the adjective or by using 'most'; in French, we use **le plus**, **la plus**, or **les plus**:

**Pierre est le plus petit de la classe.**
Pierre is the smallest in the class.
**Annette est la plus grande de la famille.**
Annette is the tallest in the family.
**Pierre et Nicole sont les plus intelligents du groupe.**
Pierre and Nicole are the most intelligent in the group.
**Michel est le plus jeune pilote de la compagnie aérienne.**
Michel is the youngest pilot in the airline company.

Note that 'in' is translated **de** after a superlative.

If the adjective is one that normally follows the noun, **le/la/les** are placed both before and after the noun:

**le vin le plus cher**
the dearest wine
**les livres les plus intéressants**
the most interesting books

## 40 SUPERLATIVE OF ADVERBS

With adverbs we use the masculine form **le plus**, even if the person or thing carrying out the action is feminine:

**Annette travaille le plus rapidement de tous.**
Annette works the fastest of all.

## 41 BETTER, BEST, WORSE, WORST

There are a few irregular comparisons and superlatives:

| bon (good) | meilleur (better) | le meilleur (the best) |
|---|---|---|
| bonne | meilleure | la meilleure (f.) |

mauvais (bad) pire (worse)    le pire (the worst)

Note that **plus mauvais** and **le plus mauvais** are also possible and, in fact, are more usual.

| bien (well) | mieux (better) | le mieux (the best) |
|---|---|---|
| peu (little) | moins (less) | le moins (the least) |
| beaucoup (much) | plus (more) | le plus (the most) |

Examples:

| Un bon restaurant. | A good restaurant. |
|---|---|
| Un meilleur restaurant. | A better restaurant. |
| Le meilleur restaurant. | The best restaurant. |
| Je chante bien. | I sing well. |
| Vous chantez mieux. | You sing better. |
| Il chante le mieux de tous. | He sings the best of all. |

6

### VOCABULARY

| le parc | park |
|---|---|
| le monde | world |
| la ville | town |
| chic | smart |
| célèbre | famous |
| agréable | pleasant |
| confortable | comfortable |
| impressionnant | impressive |

## Exercise 32

Respond to each sentence with the superlative:

Ce parc est grand. This park is large.
Oui, c'est le plus grand parc du monde.
Yes, this is the largest park in the world.

1 Ce restaurant est chic.
2 Cette librairie est grande.
3 Ce magasin est célèbre.
4 Cette cathédrale est belle.
5 Cette bière est bonne.
6 Ce parc est agréable.
7 Londres est une ville intéressante.
8 La Cadillac est une voiture confortable.
9 Le '747' est un avion impressionnant.

# 6

## 42 TALKING ABOUT THE WEATHER

The French often discuss the weather. The verb **faire**
appears in many expressions connected with this topic:

| | |
|---|---|
| **Il fait beau.** | The weather is fine. |
| **Il fait mauvais.** | The weather is bad. |
| **Il fait chaud.** | It's hot. |
| **Il fait froid.** | It's cold. |
| **Il fait du vent.** | It's windy. |
| **Il fait du soleil.** | It's sunny. |
| **Il fait du brouillard.** | It's foggy. |
| **Il pleut.** | It's raining. |
| **Il neige.** | It's snowing. |

## Exercise 33

Which French expression describes the weather in the following situations?

**1** An umbrella would be useful.

**2** Due to poor visibility, there could be some road accidents.

**3** Hold on to your hat!

**4** You'll need a warm overcoat.

**5** Dark glasses would be a great help.

**6** It's nice when this happens at Christmas.

**7** Open the window and let in a little cool air.

**8** Probably best to stay at home.

**9** A walk through the park would be pleasant.

## 43  VERBS FORMING THE PAST WITH 'ÊTRE'

6

We saw in section 17 that the past tense of most French verbs is formed with **avoir** (to have):

**j'ai téléphoné**   I telephoned
**vous avez fini**   you finished

But some verbs, often denoting motion, form their past with **être**. The following verbs, some of which are irregular, are the most important:

**aller (irreg.)**      to go
**arriver**             to arrive
**retourner**           to return
**monter**              to go up to
**rester**              stay
**partir (irreg.)**     to leave
**sortir (irreg.)**     to go out
**venir (irreg.)**      to come
**revenir (irreg.)**    to come back
**descendre**           to go down

Examples:
**je suis allé**    I went
**je suis arrivé**    I arrived
**il est parti**    he left
**il est sorti**    he went out
**vous êtes venu**    you came
**vous êtes descendu**    you went down

NOTE: When **monter** and **descendre** mean, respectively, 'to take up' and 'to bring down', they form the perfect tense with **avoir** (see Exercise 23).

The past participles (**allé**, **parti**, **venu**, etc) of these verbs agree in gender and number with the person carrying out the action (the subject), just as if they were adjectives:

masculine singular
**je suis allé**
**il est arrivé**
**vous êtes retourné**
**tu es resté**

feminine singular
**je suis partie**
**elle est sortie**
**vous êtes venue**
**tu es descendue**

masculine plural
**nous sommes allés**
**vous êtes partis**
**ils sont revenus**

feminine plural
**nous sommes restées**
**vous êtes sorties**
**elles sont descendues**

## VOCABULARY

| | | | |
|---|---|---|---|
| **le bureau** | office | **tout (m.)** | all |
| **l'étudiant (m.)** | student | **tous (m. pl.)** | |
| **la réunion** | meeting | **toute (f.)** | |
| **la journée** | day (daytime) | **toutes (f. pl.)** | |
| **la maison** | house, home | | |
| **l'infirmière (f.)** | nurse | | |
| **l'étudiante (f.)** | student | | |

## Exercise 34

**A** Imagine for a moment the following:

You are a doctor (male). You arrived at the hospital this morning at 7 o'clock. You went to a meeting at 10 o'clock. You left the hospital with two nurses.

Now complete these sentences:

1 Je suis (doctor).
2 Ce matin je (arriver) à l'hôpital à 7 heures.
3 Je (aller) à une réunion à 10 heures.
4 Je (partir) avec deux infirmières.

**B** Imagine the following:

You are a journalist (female). Yesterday you went to a press conference. At one o'clock you went upstairs to the restaurant. You returned to the office very late.

Now complete these sentences:

1 Je suis (journalist).
2 Hier je (aller) à une conférence de presse.
3 Je (monter) au restaurant à une heure.
4 Je (retourner) au bureau très tard.

**C** Consider the following:

Nicole and Sophie are students. They went to the university this morning at 9 o'clock. They stayed the whole day in the library. They came back home at 5 o'clock.

Now complete these sentences:

1 Nicole et Sophie sont (students).
2 Ce matin elles (aller) à l'université à 9 heures.
3 Elles (rester) toute la journée à la bibliothèque.
4 Elles (revenir) à la maison à 5 heures.

## VOCABULARY

| | |
|---|---|
| l'ingénieur (m.) | engineer |
| hier | yesterday |
| déjà | already |
| tôt | early |

### Exercise 35

Translate:

1 The engineers arrived yesterday.
2 The nurses (f.) have already left.
3 We (f.) came back early.
4 You (fam. sing. m.) went downstairs.
5 Did the doctor stay all day?
6 Did you come back very late?

## 44 THE USEFUL EXPRESSION 'JE VOUDRAIS'

You will want to ask for things and to say what you would like to do. Use **je voudrais** (I would like):

**Je voudrais un café.**
I'd like a coffee.
**Je voudrais de la confiture.**
I'd like some jam.
**Je voudrais prendre le petit déjeuner dans ma chambre.**
I would like to have (take) breakfast in my room.
**Je voudrais rester deux jours.**
I would like to stay two days.

NOTE

**1** If you ask for **un café**, you will receive black coffee; if you want white coffee, ask for **un café crème** or, at breakfast time, **un café au lait**.

**2** **voudrais** is actually the conditional tense, which we shall be studying later.

## VOCABULARY

| | |
|---|---|
| **le timbre** | stamp |
| **le plan** | street map |
| **le lait** | milk |
| **le sucre** | sugar |
| **le thé** | tea |
| **la carte postale** | postcard |
| **la note** | bill (in a hotel) |
| **l'addition (f.)** | bill (in a restaurant) |
| **régler** | settle |

## IRREGULAR VERB

**envoyer** (to send)

Present tense
**j'envoie**
**tu envoies**
**il/elle envoie**
**nous envoyons**
**vous envoyez**
**ils/elles envoient**

## Exercise 36

Ask for the following, using je voudrais:

1 a postcard
2 a stamp
3 a street map of the town
4 an American newspaper
5 some milk
6 some sugar
7 some tea

And now, say that you would like:

7 to telephone New York
8 to settle the hotel bill

## 6 45 USINGTHE EXPRESSION 'IL FAUT' (ONE MUST)

If you want to say that something has to be done, you can use **il faut** (one must, it is necessary):

**Il faut conduire à droite.**
You have to drive on the right.
**Il faut aller à la pharmacie.**
You have to go to the chemist's.

Also note this useful way of talking about what you need:

**Il nous faut un dictionnaire.**
We need a dictionary (it is necessary to us a dictionary).

| | |
|---|---|
| **le crayon** | pencil |
| **le stylo-bille** | ball-point pen |
| **le papier à lettres** | writing paper |
| **la gomme** | eraser |
| **l'enveloppe (f.)** | envelope |
| **l'allumette (f.)** | match |

## Exercise 37

Say you need the following:

1 a pencil
2 a ball-point pen

Now, she needs:

3 a rubber
4 some writing paper

Now, they need:

5 some envelopes
6 some cigarettes
7 some matches

6

| | |
|---|---|
| **le port** | port |
| **le pain** | bread |
| **l'article (m.)** | item |
| **la place** | square |
| **la rue** | street |
| **la marque** | brand |
| **la promotion** | special offer |
| **la porte** | door |
| **l'année (f.)** | year |
| **tourner** | to turn |
| **recommander** | to recommend |
| **tout droit** | straight on |
| **à gauche** | on/to the left |
| **à droite** | on/to the right |
| **d'habitude** | usually |
| **au revoir** | goodbye |
| **si** | so |
| **voilà** | there is (pointing) |
| **autre** | other |
| **rouge** | red |
| **quelques** | a few |
| **dernier,** | |
| **dernière (f.)** | last |

**6**

*Un touriste passe la journée à Boulogne*

TOURISTE **Pardon, Madame. Je cherche une bonne épicerie, ici près du port.**

PASSANTE **La meilleure épicerie de Boulogne est sur la place, en face de la banque. Vous allez tout droit et vous prenez la première rue à gauche.**

TOURISTE **Merci, Madame. [Il répète] ... je vais tout droit, je tourne à droite ... non, non ... je tourne à gauche. Ah, voilà l'épicerie.**

EPICIÈRE **Bonjour, Monsieur. Vous désirez?**

TOURISTE **Bonjour, Madame. Je voudrais du fromage, du vin et de la bière, s'il vous plaît.**

EPICIÈRE **Voici le fromage. C'est la meilleure marque. Il est plus cher que les autres fromages, mais il est excellent. Je vous recommande aussi ce vin rouge. Il est moins cher que d'habitude; il est en promotion.**

TOURISTE **Bien. Je prends ces trois articles. Merci. Est-ce que vous vendez aussi du pain?**

EPICIÈRE **Non, Monsieur. Pour cela, il faut aller à la boulangerie. La boulangerie est à côté du bureau de poste.**

TOURISTE **Merci. Au revoir, Madame. [Il va à la porte] ... Oh, il pleut! Et il fait du vent.**

EPICIÈRE **Attendez quelques instants. Ici à Boulogne il fait rarement beau. Il pleut souvent et il fait toujours du vent.**

TOURISTE **Oui. L'année dernière ma femme et moi, nous sommes venus passer la journée ici, mais il a fait si mauvais. Nous avons attendu un jour, deux jours.**
**Finalement, nous sommes restés une semaine à Boulogne!**

**6**

*A tourist spends the day in Boulogne*

TOURIST  Excuse me. I'm looking for a good food store, here near the port.

PASSER-BY  The best food store in Boulogne is in (on) the square, opposite the bank. You go straight on and you take the first street on the left.

TOURIST  Thank you. [He repeats] ... I go straight on, I turn right ... no, no ... I turn left. Ah, there's the food store.

STOREKEEPER  Good morning, Sir. What would you like? [Literally 'you wish?']

TOURIST  Good morning. I'd like some cheese, some wine, and some beer, please.

STOREKEEPER  Here's the cheese. It's the best brand. It's dearer than the other cheeses, but it's excellent. I also recommend this red wine. It's less expensive than usual; it's a special offer.

TOURIST  Fine. I'll take [literally 'I take'] these three items. Thank you. Do you sell bread?

STOREKEEPER  No, Sir. For that you have to go to the baker's. The baker's is next to the post office.

TOURIST  Thank you. [He goes to the door]... Oh, it's raining. And it's windy.

STOREKEEPER  Wait a few moments. Here in Boulogne the weather's rarely fine. It often rains and it's always windy.

TOURIST  Yes. Last year my wife and I came to spend the day here, but the weather was so bad. We waited ... We waited one day, two days. Finally, we stayed in Boulogne for a week!

6

# Week 7

- adverbs of quantity (much, many, enough, etc)
- the future tense (including the irregular forms of some key verbs' )
- the all-important modal verbs 'pouvoir', 'devoir', 'vouloir' and 'savoir'
- countries
- more numbers (up to 100)
- four more irregular verbs

## 46 QUANTITY: MUCH, MANY, ENOUGH, ETC

On occasions, you will need to talk about quantities – you may have too much of something, or too little, or not enough, and so on.

Study the following:

| | |
|---|---|
| **beaucoup** | much, many |
| **trop** | too much, too many |
| **tant** | so much, so many |
| **peu** | little, few |
| **assez** | enough |

When a noun follows these words, they are linked by **de (d')**:

| | |
|---|---|
| **beaucoup de temps (m.)** | much time |
| **beaucoup de légumes (m.)** | many vegetables |
| **trop d'argent** | too much money |
| **trop de vêtements (m.)** | too many clothes |
| **peu de patience (f.)** | little patience |
| **assez de fruits (m. pl.)** | enough fruit |

The following are also linked to the noun by **de (d')**:

| | |
|---|---|
| **plus** | more |
| **moins** | less, fewer |
| **autant** | as much, as many |

Examples:

**J'ai l'intention de boire plus d'eau.**
I intend to drink more water.
**J'ai l'intention de manger moins de pain.**
I intend to eat less bread.
**Rémi a autant de CD que Marie-Claude.**
Rémi has as many CDs as Marie-Claude.

## VOCABULARY

| | |
|---|---|
| **le chapeau** | hat |
| **le pantalon** | pair of trousers |
| **le foulard** | scarf |
| **le cardigan** | cardigan |
| **le costume** | suit |
| **la chemise** | shirt |
| **la cravate** | tie |
| **la robe** | dress |
| **la jupe** | skirt |

7

# Exercise 38

Answer the questions.

Example:
Vous faut-il une chemise? Do you need a shirt?
Non, j'ai beaucoup de chemises. No, I have many shirts.

1 Vous faut-il une cravate?

2 Vous faut-il un costume?

3 Vous faut-il une robe?

Example:
Michel a acheté un chapeau? Has Michel bought a hat?
Oui, il a maintenant trop de chapeaux. Yes, he now has too many hats.

4 Bernard a acheté un pantalon?

5 Hélène a acheté une jupe?

6 Marie-José a acheté un foulard?

Translate:

7 He has little patience.

8 Have you put enough shirts in the suitcase?

9 I have more cardigans than Monique.

10 You have fewer suits than Pierre.

7

You will often want to talk about what you plan to do in the future. There are three ways of doing this:

**1** In conversation, you can often use the present tense with a future meaning:

**Un petit instant, je finis ce rapport.**
One moment, I'll just finish this report.
**Bien. Je prends ces trois articles.**
Fine. I'll take these three items.
**J'arrive lundi.**
I'll arrive on Monday.

**2** You can do what we do in English, i.e. use 'to go', followed by another verb:

**Je vais téléphoner demain.**
I'm going to telephone tomorrow.
**Aujourd'hui il va manger dans un restaurant chic.**
Today he's going to eat in a smart restaurant.
**Nous allons regarder la télévision ce soir.**
We're going to watch television this evening.

**3** You can use the future tense which is formed by adding the following endings to the infinitive of the verb:

| | |
|---|---|
| **je** | **- ai** |
| **tu** | **- as** |
| **il/elle** | **- a** |
| **nous** | **- ons** |
| **vous** | **- ez** |
| **ils/elles** | **- ont** |

Examples:
| | |
|---|---|
| **je consulterai** | I will consult |
| **tu chanteras** | you (fam.) will sing |
| **il fumera** | he will smoke |

| | |
|---|---|
| **elle exportera** | she will export |
| **nous choisirons** | we will choose |
| **vous finirez** | you will finish |
| **ils garantiront** | they will guarantee |
| **elles réussiront** | they (f.) will succeed |

To form the future of **-re** verbs, drop the final **e** of the infinitive before adding the endings:

| | |
|---|---|
| **j'attendrai** | I will wait |
| **il apprendra** | he will learn |
| **nous comprendrons** | we will understand |
| **vous mettrez** | you will put |
| **ils promettront** | they will promise |

Some important verbs have an irregular future and perhaps we should learn them now:

| | | |
|---|---|---|
| **avoir** | **j'aurai** | I will have |
| **être** | **je serai** | I will be |
| **aller** | **j'irai** | I will go |
| **faire** | **je ferai** | I will do, make |

| | | |
|---|---|---|
| **venir** | **je viendrai** | I will come |
| **envoyer** | **j'enverrai** | I will send |

| | | |
|---|---|---|
| **il y a** | **il y aura** | there will be |
| **il faut** | **il faudra** | it will be necessary |

7

## VOCABULARY

| | |
|---|---|
| le tennis | tennis |
| le week-end | weekend |
| le père | father |
| l'appartement (m.) | flat |
| la réunion | meeting |
| la conférence | conference |
| la mère | mother |
| les courses (f.) | shopping |
| international | international |
| étudier | to study |
| réparer | to repair |
| jouer | to play |
| visiter | to visit |
| tapisser | to wallpaper |
| organiser | to organise |

## IRREGULAR VERB

**écrire** (to write)

Present tense
**j'écris**
**tu écris**
**il/elle écrit**
**nous écrivons**
**vous écrivez**
**ils/elles écrivent**

Perfect tense
**j'ai écrit**, etc

## Exercise 39

Here is a list of things you plan to do tomorrow (**demain**). Translate the list into French, using the construction with **aller**. Write complete sentences.

1 Listen to radio
2 Buy newspaper
3 Study French
4 Do shopping

Here is Michel's list for next week (**la semaine prochaine**). Translate, using the future tense in complete sentences:

5 Repair car
6 Play tennis
7 Write letter
8 Visit museum

Here is Pierre and Hélène's list for next month (**le mois prochain**). Use the future tense, and write complete sentences:

9 Wallpaper flat
10 Organise meeting
11 Go to international conference
12 Spend weekend in London

Translate:

13 She will finish her letter.
14 We will go to the theatre next week.
15 You will surprise your father.
16 You (fam.) will choose your dress next month.

**CAN, MUST, WANT, KNOW (MODAL VERBS)**

These are auxiliary verbs that are used in conjunction with the infinitive of a following verb – for example, 'I can come' or 'We must telephone'. There are four important examples of this type of verb in French:

**pouvoir**  to be able to (can)
**devoir**  to have to (must)
**vouloir**  to want to
**savoir**  to know (know how to)

### 1 Pouvoir
Sometimes you will want to talk about what you can or cannot do. Use the irregular verb **pouvoir**:

Present tense: I can, etc
**je peux**
**tu peux**
**il/elle peut**
**nous pouvons**
**vous pouvez**
**ils/elles peuvent**

Past tense (perfect):
**j'ai pu,** I was able to

Future tense
**je pourrai,** I will be able to

Examples:
**Je peux faire les courses maintenant.**
I can do the shopping now.
**Pouvez-vous me dire où est la gare?**
Can you tell me where the station is?
**Avez-vous pu téléphoner à Paris ?**
Have you been able to telephone Paris?

In formal situations **puis-je** is sometimes used in place of **est-ce que je peux** to express 'can I . . .?'
or 'may I . . .?'

**2 Devoir**

You will also want to talk about what you must or have to do. Use the irregular verb devoir:

Present tense: I must, etc
**je dois**
**tu dois**
**il/elle doit**
**nous devons**
**vous devez**
**ils/elles doivent**

Past tense (perfect)
**j'ai dû** I had to

Future tense
**je devrai** I will have to

Examples:
**Je dois changer ma vie.**
I must change my life.
**Vous devez envoyer une carte postale à votre ami.**
You must send a postcard to your friend.
**Il a dû partir.**
He had to leave.
**Elle devra apprendre l'espagnol.**
She will have to learn Spanish.

**3 Vouloir**

You have already met **je voudrais** meaning 'I would like'; this comes from the irregular verb **vouloir** (to want):

Present tense: I want, etc
**je veux**
**tu veux**
**il/elle veut**
**nous voulons**
**vous voulez**
**ils/elles veulent**

Past tense (perfect)
**j'ai voulu** I wanted

Future tense
**je voudrai** I will want

Examples:
**Je veux changer mon argent américain en euros.**
I want to change my American money into euros.
**Nous voulons une chambre pour deux personnes.**
We want a double room.

A request can be made more polite by putting
'**Voulez-vous . . .**' at the beginning of the sentence:
**Voulez-vous signer ici?** Will you sign here?

**4 Savoir**
The irregular verb savoir means 'to know':

Present tense: I know, etc
**je sais**
**tu sais**
**il/elle sait**
**nous savons**
**vous savez**
**ils/elles savent**

Past tense (perfect)
**j'ai su** I knew

Future tense
**je saurai** I will know

Examples:
**Je sais que vous voyagez à l'étranger.**
I know that you travel abroad.
**Savez-vous où je peux louer une voiture?**
Do you know where I can hire a car?
**Pierre saura demain s'il va être en chômage.**
Pierre will know tomorrow if he's going to be
unemployed (lit. 'in unemployment')

**Savoir** can also mean 'to know how to':

**Je sais jouer du piano.**
I can (know how to) play the piano.

Note the difference between **pouvoir** and **savoir**:

**Je ne sais pas jouer du piano.**
I can't play the piano. (I don't know how to)
**Je ne peux pas jouer du piano.**
I can't play the piano. (my hand is bandaged)

## VOCABULARY

| | |
|---|---|
| **le diplomate** | diplomat |
| **le marché** | market |
| **le contrat** | contract |
| **l'écriture (f.)** | handwriting |
| **arrêter** | to stop |
| **arrêter de fumer** | to stop smoking |
| **décourager** | to discourage |
| **nager** | to swim |
| **garer** | to park |
| **faire le tour** | to tour the world |
| **du monde** | |

### IRREGULAR VERB

**conduire** (to drive)

Present tense
**je conduis**
**tu conduis**
**il/elle conduit**
**nous conduisons**
**vous conduisez**
**ils/elles conduisent**

Perfect tense
**j'ai conduit**, etc

7

## Exercise 40

Say that you can:

1 buy the vegetables at the market
2 prepare the report

Say that we cannot:

3 arrive on Monday
4 read his handwriting

Say that she must:

5 sign the contract
6 stop smoking

Say that they must not:

7 discourage the students
8 park the car in front of the hospital

Say that he wants to:

9 tour the world
10 spend less money

Ask your friend whether he/she knows how to:

11 drive
12 swim

In French, countries can be either masculine or feminine:

| | |
|---|---|
| **le Danemark** | Denmark |
| **le Portugal** | Portugal |
| **le Luxembourg** | Luxemburg |
| **le Canada** | Canada |
| **le Japon** | Japan |
| **le Pays de Galles** | Wales |
| **les États-Unis (m.)** | United States |
| **le Royaume-Uni** | United Kingdom |
| **la France** | France |
| **la Belgique** | Belgium |
| **la Grande-Bretagne** | Great Britain |
| **la Grèce** | Greece |
| **la Hollande** | Holland |
| **la Chine** | China |
| **la Russie** | Russia |
| **l'Angleterre (f.)** | England |
| **l'Ecosse (f.)** | Scotland |
| **l'Allemagne (f.)** | Germany |
| **l'Italie (f.)** | Italy |
| **l'Espagne (f.)** | Spain |
| **l'Irlande (f.)** | Ireland |

Before a masculine country 'in' or 'to' is translated **au**:

| | |
|---|---|
| **au Pays de Galles** | in/to Wales |
| **au Portugal** | in/to Portugal |
| **au Japon** | in/to Japan |

Before a feminine country 'in' or 'to' is translated **en**:

| | |
|---|---|
| **en Angleterre** | in/to England |
| **en Écosse** | in/to Scotland |
| **en France** | in/to France |
| **en Chine** | in/to China |

We use aux for a country with a plural form:

| | |
|---|---|
| **aux États-Unis** | in/to the United States |

7

## Exercise 41

With your book closed, write a list of 15 countries, indicating whether they are masculine or feminine. Then check your list against the lists above.

## Exercise 42

Translate:

1 We spend our holidays in Greece.
2 Do you intend to go to Japan?
3 Germany exports cars to France.
4 Has the diplomat arrived in Russia?

## 50 NUMBERS

Let's continue our study of the numbers:

| | | | |
|---|---|---|---|
| 63 | soixante-trois | 81 | quatre-vingt-un |
| 70 | soixante-dix | 82 | quatre-vingt-deux |
| 71 | soixante et onze | 88 | quatre-vingt-huit |
| 72 | soixante-douze | 90 | quatre-vingt-dix |
| 73 | soixante-treize | 91 | quatre-vingt-onze |
| 79 | soixante-dix-neuf | 99 | quatre-vingt-dix-neuf |
| 80 | quatre-vingts | 100 | cent |

Note that the **s** in **quatre-vingts** is omitted when another number follows.

7

## Exercise 43

Complete the following, writing the answers in words:

a  10 + 10 =          g  40 + 30 =

b  10 + 12 =          h  19 + 60 =

c  11 + 20 =          i  40 + 41 =

d  27 + 20 =          j  41 + 50 =

e  30 + 29 =          k  19 + 80 =

f  21 + 40 =          l  50 + 50 =

## VOCABULARY

| | |
|---|---|
| la résolution | resolution |
| la liste | list |
| la promesse | promise |
| la gymnastique | physical exercises |
| la santé | health |
| certain | certain |
| neuf, neuve (f.) | brand-new |
| quoi | what |
| quoi de neuf? | what's new? |
| eh bien? | well? |
| vraiment | really |
| ça = cela | that |
| souhaiter | to wish |
| décider (de) | to decide (to) |
| excuser | to excuse |

## IRREGULAR VERBS

**boire** (to drink)        **dire** (to say, to tell)

Present tense              Present tense
**je bois**                **je dis**
**tu bois**                **tu dis**
**il/elle boit**           **il/elle dit**
**nous buvons**            **nous disons**
**vous buvez**             **vous dites**
**ils/elles boivent**      **ils/elles disent**

Perfect tense              Perfect tense
**j'ai bu**, etc           **j'ai dit**, etc

## CONVERSATION

*Hélène prend des résolutions pour la nouvelle année*

MICHEL **Bonjour, Hélène. Je suis venu vous souhaiter une bonne année.**

HÉLÈNE **Bonjour, Michel. Bonne année à vous aussi.**

MICHEL **Quoi de neuf?**

HÉLÈNE **Eh bien, j'ai décidé de changer ma vie. J'ai pris beaucoup de résolutions pour la nouvelle année.**

MICHEL **Vraiment? Et quelles sont ces résolutions?**

HÉLÈNE **Voici ma liste:**
**1 Je vais maigrir.**
**2 Je vais regarder la télévision moins souvent.**
**3 Je mangerai plus de légumes.**
**4 Je mangerai plus de fruits.**
**5 Je dépenserai moins d'argent en vêtements.**
**Mon mari m'a fait aussi quelques promesses. Voici sa liste:**
**1 Il va boire moins de bière.**
**2 Il va boire plus d'eau.**
**3 Il arrêtera de fumer.**
**4 Il fera de la gymnastique chaque matin.**
**5 Il rentrera plus tôt à la maison le soir.**

MICHEL **Et vous pensez que vous serez plus heureux?**

HÉLÈNE **Oui. Nous aurons plus de temps et plus d'argent. Nous serons tous les deux en meilleure santé.**

MICHEL **Et comment est-ce que vous dépenserez tout et argent?**

HÉLÈNE **Nous achèterons une voiture neuve. Nous voyagerons à l'étranger plus souvent. Nous irons au Japon. Nous irons en Chine et aux États-Unis. Nous ferons le tour du monde.**

MICHEL **Excusez-moi, mais je dois dire que j'ai déjà entendu ça. Je l'ai entendu l'année dernière. Je ne veux pas vous décourager, mais je suis certain que vous ne ferez jamais rien !**

## TRANSLATION

*Hélène makes [takes] some New Year resolutions*

MICHEL   Good morning, Hélène. I've come to wish you a happy New Year.

HÉLÈNE   Good morning, Michel. Happy New Year to you too.

MICHEL   What's new?

HÉLÈNE   Well, I've decided to change my life. I've made a lot of resolutions for the New Year.

MICHEL   Really? And what are these resolutions?

HÉLÈNE   Here's my list:

1 I'm going to lose weight.
2 I'm going to watch television less often.
3 I'll eat more vegetables.
4 I'll eat more fruit.
5 I'll spend less money on [literally 'in'] clothes.

My husband has also made me a few promises. Here's his list:

1 He's going to drink less beer.
2 He's going to drink more water.
3 He'll stop smoking.
4 He'll do exercises each morning.
5 He'll come home earlier in the evening.

MICHEL   Do you think you'll be happier?

HÉLÈNE   Yes. We'll have more time and more money. We'll both [literally 'all the two'] be in better health.

MICHEL   And how will you spend all this money?

HÉLÈNE   We'll buy a brand-new car. We'll travel abroad more often. We'll go to Japan. We'll go to China and to the United States. We'll tour the world [literally 'We'll do the tour of the world'].

MICHEL   I'm sorry [literally 'Excuse me'] but I have to say that I've heard all that before [literally I've already heard that]. I heard it last year. I don't want to discourage you, but I'm sure that you'll never do anything! [literally 'that you will never do nothing'].

# Week 8

- *the imperfect tense ('used to do', 'was doing')*
- *relative pronouns (who/whom/which/that)*
- *the conditional tense ('what we would do, if ...')*
- *more about pronouns*
- *the distinction between 'savoir' and 'connaître', both meaning 'to know'*

## 51 THE IMPERFECT TENSE ('USED TO DO', 'WAS DOING')

We have already used the perfect tense to talk about the past:

**J'ai acheté un livre.**

This sentence can be translated by 'I have bought a book', 'I did buy a book', or 'I bought a book'.

But sometimes you want to say what you 'used to do' at some period in your life. For this you use the imperfect tense. To form this tense, take the **nous** form of the present tense, drop the **-ons** ending and add:

| je | - ais | nous | - ions |
|---|---|---|---|
| tu | - ais | vous | - iez |
| il/elle | - ait | ils/elles | - aient |

There is only one exception to the above rule, namely the verb **être**.

Examples:

| | |
|---|---|
| **je fumais** | I used to smoke |
| **tu chantais** | you (fam.) used to sing |
| **il organisait** | he used to organise |
| **elle choisissait** | she used to choose |
| **nous finissions** | we used to finish |
| **vous vendiez** | you used to sell |
| **ils lisaient** | they used to read |
| **elles écrivaient** | they used to write |

**j'étais**   I used to be (was)
**il était**   he used to be (was)
etc

**j'avais**   I used to have (had)
**il avait**   he used to have (had)
etc

We also use the imperfect tense when translating such sentences as 'I was reading the newspaper, when the telephone rang.' In other words, if the English construction is 'was/were …ing', we require the imperfect tense in French.

Examples:
**J'écoutais la radio, quand Michel a téléphoné.**
I was listening to the radio when Michel telephoned.
**Elle prenait une douche, quand le facteur est arrivé.**
She was taking a shower when the postman arrived.

## VOCABULARY

| | |
|---|---|
| **le timbre** | stamp |
| **le bruit** | noise |
| **le porte-monnaie** | purse |
| **le cambrioleur** | burglar |
| **la traduction** | translation |
| **en haut** | upstairs |
| **en bas** | downstairs |
| **collectionner** | to collect |
| **jouer au football** | to play football |
| **aller à la pêche** | to go fishing |
| **faire de la photo(graphie)** | to do photography |
| **entrer dans la maison** | to enter the house |

8

## Exercise 44

Here are some things that Bernard and Marie-Claude used to do when they were younger; translate using the imperfect tense:

1 He used to play football.
2 He used to go fishing.
3 He used to collect stamps.
4 She used to sing.
5 She used to listen to records.

Now translate:

6 We used to learn Spanish.
7 We used to live in a small house.
8 We used to go in for photography.
9 I was finishing the translation, when I heard a noise upstairs.
10 She was doing the shopping, when she lost her purse.
11 They were watching television, when the burglar entered the house.

## 8

### 52 RELATIVE PRONOUNS: WHO, WHOM, WHICH, THAT

Study the following:

**qui**  who, which, that (subject)
**que**  whom, which, that (object)

Note: **que** becomes **qu'** in front of a vowel or h.

Examples:
**L'automobiliste qui parle français.**
The motorist who speaks French.
**La voiture qui est en panne (f.).**
The car which has broken down
(lit. 'which is in breakdown').

**L'auto-stoppeur que j'ai pris.**
The hitch-hiker whom I picked up.
**Le camion que vous avez réparé.**
The lorry which you repaired.

If you're having difficulty in deciding whether 'who', 'which', 'that' is the subject or the object, here's a rule to help you:

if, in English, the verb comes immediately after 'who', 'which', 'that', use **qui**;
if, in English, there is another word between 'who', 'which', 'that', and the verb, use **que**

Examples:
the car which has broken down       **qui**
the car which I prefer              **que**

NOTE: In English, 'whom', 'which', and 'that' are sometimes omitted, but they must always be expressed in French:

**Le moteur que vous vérifiez.**
The engine you are checking.

We learnt in section 34 that in the perfect tense the verb (**invité**, **copié**, **trouvé**) has to reflect the gender and number of pronouns such as 'me' or 'him' which are used with it; the same principle applies to **que**:

**Voici le permis de conduire que j'ai trouvé.**
Here is the driving licence that I found.
**Voici la carte que j'ai achetée.**
Here's the map that I bought.
**Voici les pneus que j'ai choisis.**
Here are the tyres which I've chosen.

After a preposition, 'whom' is also translated by **qui**:

**Où est le mécanicien à qui vous avez téléphoné?**
Where's the mechanic to whom you telephoned?
(Where's the mechanic you telephoned?)

8

BUT 'which', after prepositions, is translated as follows:

**lequel (m.)**  **lesquels (m. pl. .)**
**laquelle (f.)**  **lesquelles (f. pl.)**

The above words combine with **à** and **de** in the usual way: **auquel, duquel, desquels, desquelles**.

For example:
**Le cric avec lequel il a changé la roue.**
The jack with which he changed the wheel.
**La galerie sur laquelle nous avons mis les valises.**
The roof rack on which we put the suitcases.
**Le garage auquel elle a envoyé son chèque.**
The garage to which she sent her cheque.

In place of **de qui, duquel, de laquelle, desquels, desquelles**, the French often prefer to use **dont**:

**L'autoroute dont nous parlons.**
The motorway which we are speaking of (about).

We also use **dont** to mean 'whose':

**L'automobiliste dont la femme est malade.**
The motorist whose wife is ill.
**Le garagiste dont je connais le frère.**
The garage owner whose brother I know.

Note the unexpected word order in the last French sentence.

Also note the way the French use **ce qui** (subject) or **ce que** (object) where the English use 'what' as a link word:

**Je ne peux pas lire ce qui est écrit ici.**
I cannot read what is written here.
**Je ne peux pas lire ce que Michel a écrit ici.**
I cannot read what Michel has written here.

## VOCABULARY

| | |
|---|---|
| **le petit déjeuner** | breakfast |
| **le poste de télévision** | television set |
| **le vestibule** | hall |
| **le/la réceptionniste** | receptionist |
| **le fils** | son |
| **l'ascenseur (m.)** | lift |
| **la femme de chambre** | chambermaid |
| **la fille** | daughter, girl |
| **lourd** | heavy |
| **bilingue** | bilingual |
| **malade** | ill |
| **correct** | correct |
| **apporter** | to bring |
| **commander** | to order |
| **marcher** | to walk, to work (machines) |
| **donner sur** | to overlook |

## Exercise 45

Translate:

1 The hotel that you are looking for is on the right.

2 I would like the room which overlooks the park.

3 The room, which we have reserved for you, is next to the lift.

4 I've brought the breakfast that your husband ordered.

5 Where's the television set which doesn't work?

6 The suitcases, which are in the hall, are very heavy.

7 The receptionist (f.), to whom you spoke, is bilingual.

8 The client, whose son is ill, is in room 5.

9 Didn't you understand what the chambermaid said to you?

10 The bill, that you have prepared, is correct.

8

## 53 THE CONDITIONAL TENSE ('WHAT WE WOULD DO IF ...')

We form the conditional tense by adding the following endings to the infinitive of the verb:

| | | | |
|---|---|---|---|
| **je** | **-ais** | **nous** | **-ions** |
| **tu** | **-ais** | **vous** | **-iez** |
| **il/elle** | **-ait** | **ils/elles** | **-aient** |

As with the future tense, if the infinitive ends in **-re**, omit the final **e** before adding the endings.

Examples:

| | |
|---|---|
| **je louerais** | I would hire |
| **tu inviterais** | you (fam.) would invite |
| **il habiterait** | he would live |
| **elle étudierait** | she would study |
| **nous choisirions** | we would choose |
| **vous finiriez** | you would finish |
| **ils comprendraient** | they would understand |
| **elles écriraient** | they would write |

When a verb is irregular in the future tense, it will have the same irregularity in the conditional tense:

| | |
|---|---|
| **j'aurais** | I would have |
| **tu serais** | you (fam.) would be |
| **il irait** | he would go |
| **elle ferait** | she would do |
| **nous enverrions** | we would send |
| **vous pourriez** | you could, would be able |
| **ils voudraient** | they would like |
| **elles sauraient** | they would know |
| **il faudrait** | it would be necessary |
| **il y aurait** | there would be |

The 'if' part of the sentence (i.e. 'if I had the time', 'if I spoke French', etc) is expressed by **si** (if) and the imperfect:

8

**si j'avais le temps** if I had the time
**s'il parlait français** if he spoke French
**si vous vendiez votre maison** if you sold your house

Note: **si** becomes **s'** before **il** and **ils**.

The conditional is also used in French when the speaker or writer is repeating something he or she has heard but is unable to vouch for its accuracy. Compare:

**Le père a donné son consentement au mariage.**
The father has given his consent to the marriage.
**Le père aurait donné son consentement au mariage.**
Apparently, the father has given his consent to
the marriage.

## VOCABULARY

| | |
|---|---|
| **le travail** | work |
| **l'interprète (m. & f.)** | interpreter |
| **l'enfant (m. & f.)** | child |
| **portugais** | Portuguese |
| **marié** | married |
| **comme** | as |
| **dessiner** | to draw |

## IRREGULAR VERB

**peindre** (to paint)

Present tense
**je peins**
**tu peins**
**il/elle peint**
**nous peignons**
**vous peignez**
**ils/elles peignent**

Perfect tense
**j'ai peint**, etc

8

## Exercise 46

Answer the questions as follows:

Qu'est-ce que vous feriez, si vous aviez beaucoup de temps?
What would you do, if you had a lot of time?
(write a book)

Si j'avais beaucoup de temps, j'écrirais un livre.
If I had a lot of time, I would write a book.

1 Qu'est-ce que vous feriez, si vous étiez riche? (tour the world)

2 Qu'est-ce que vous feriez, si vous ne travailliez pas? (paint and draw)

3 Qu'est-ce que Pierre ferait, s'il avait beaucoup de temps? (learn Portuguese)

4 Qu'est-ce que Nicole ferait, si elle parlait français? (work as an interpreter)

5 Qu'est-ce que Monique ferait, si elle parlait allemand? (work as a bilingual secretary)

6 Qu'est-ce que je ferais, si j'étais marié? (return home earlier in the evening)

7 Qu'est-ce qu'ils feraient, s'ils étaient en chômage? (look for work)

8 Qu'est-ce qu'elles feraient, si elles avaient des enfants? (stay at home)

9 Qu'est-ce que tu ferais, si tu avais le temps? (read a great deal)

10 Qu'est-ce que nous ferions, si nous voulions maigrir? (eat less and do exercises)

8

## 54 | MORE ABOUT PRONOUNS

We have already seen in week 5, section 33 how the French express 'me', 'him', 'her', 'to us', 'to you', etc, when these pronouns are the object of a verb. But some of these pronouns have a different form when they:

**1** follow a preposition
**2** form part of a comparison
**3** stand alone
**4** follow the verb **être** (to be)

Thus:

| | | | |
|---|---|---|---|
| **moi** | I, me | **nous** | we, us |
| **toi** | you (fam.) | **vous** | you |
| **lui** | he, him | **eux** | they, them (m.) |
| **elle** | she, her | **elles** | they, them (f.) |

Examples:
**Est-ce qu'il y a des lettres pour moi?**
Are there any letters for me?
**Je travaille en face de lui.**
I work opposite him.
**Nous sommes partis sans eux.**
We left without them.
**Il est plus petit que moi.**
He's smaller than I.
**Qui parle anglais ici? Elle.**
Who speaks English here? She does.
**C'est lui qui écrit toutes les lettres.**
It's he who writes all the letters.

| le président | president |
| le programmeur | computer programmer |
| le poste de radio | radio set |
| le traité | treaty |
| la femme de ménage | daily help |
| travailleur, travailleuse (f.) | hardworking |
| paresseux, paresseuse (f.) | lazy |
| casser | to break |

## Exercise 47

Replace the words in italics with a pronoun:

1 Je suis arrivé avec *Paul*.

2 Je voudrais avoir une place à côté de *la secrétaire*.

3 Nous avons l'intention de partir sans *Pierre et Monique*.

4 Anne est plus travailleuse que *les nouvelles infirmières*.

5 Michel est moins paresseux que *le nouveau programmeur*.

6 Qui a cassé mon poste de radio? *La femme de ménage*.

7 C'est *le président* et *le premier ministre* qui ont signé le traité hier.

## 55 'SAVOIR' AND 'CONNAÎTRE' ('TO KNOW')

In section 48 we learnt that 'to know' is translated by **savoir**. This verb means to know a fact:

**Savez-vous où est Paul?**
Do you know where Paul is?
**Je sais à quelle heure le train part.**
I know at what time the train leaves.

BUT, when we talk about knowing a person or a place, that is to say when the meaning is 'to be acquainted with', then we must use the irregular verb **connaître**:

Present tense
**je connais** I know, I am acquainted with
**tu connais**
**il/elle connaît**
**nous connaissons**
**vous connaissez**
**ils/elles connaissent**

Past tense (perfect)
**j'ai connu,** I knew, I was acquainted with

Examples:
**Je connais Paul, mais je ne sais pas où il habite.**
I know Paul, but I don't know where he lives.
**Vous connaissez Paris?**
Do you know Paris?

## VOCABULARY

| | |
|---|---|
| **l'oncle** | uncle |
| **libre** | free |
| **la tante** | aunt |
| **occupé** | busy |

8

## Exercise 48

Translate:

1 I don't know if Paul has finished his work.
2 I don't know the Duponts.
3 Do you know where I can hire a computer?
4 Do you know if the doctor is free?
5 Does Marie-Claude know my aunt?

In the conversation at the end of this chapter change all the familiar forms (tu, te, toi, ton) into the more formal vous/votre forms and make all necessary changes to the verbs.

## VOCABULARY

| | |
|---|---|
| le cas | case, situation |
| les gens (m. pl.) | people |
| la visite | visit |
| la porte | door |
| la retraite | retirement |
| au-dessus de | above |
| chez | at someone's home or shop |
| bonsoir | good evening |
| justement | just |
| si | so; yes (emphatic use after a negative) |
| à propos | by the way |
| à mi-temps | part time |
| tout de suite | immediately |
| trop | too |
| inattendu | unexpected |
| bruyant | noisy |
| déranger | to disturb |
| arranger | to suit |
| frapper | to knock |
| penser à | to think of (thoughts) |
| penser de | to think of (opinion) |
| espérer | to hope |

(See week 12, section 81 for how **espérer** slightly changes its spelling in the present tense.)

*Une visite inattendue*

PIERRE  **Bonsoir Nicole, j'espère que je ne te dérange pas.**

NICOLE  **Pierre! Bonsoir. Je pensais justement à toi.**

PIERRE  **Tu n'es pas trop occupée?**

NICOLE  **Non, non. J'écrivais une lettre, quand tu as frappé à la porte.**

PIERRE  **Ah bon? A qui est-ce que tu écrivais?**

NICOLE  **Aux Dupont.**

PIERRE  **Les Dupont? Je ne les connais pas.**

NICOLE  **Mais si! Les Dupont sont les gens qui habitaient au-dessus de chez nous à Paris, qui voyageaient beaucoup et dont les enfants étaient si bruyants.**

PIERRE  **Ah oui. Je ne les connaissais pas très bien. À propos, comment va ton travail?**

NICOLE  **Pas trop bien. Si seulement je pouvais travailler à mi-temps, ça m'arrangerait bien.**

PIERRE  **Qu'est-ce que tu ferais de tout ce temps libre?**

NICOLE  **Je peindrais, je dessinerais. Michel et moi, nous sortirions plus souvent, nous irions au cinéma, au restaurant. Je ferais du sport, j'apprendrais l'anglais, je lirais tous les livres que j'ai achetés l'année dernière, je ...**

PIERRE  **Tu ferais mieux de prendre ta retraite tout de suite!**

8

*An unexpected visit*

PIERRE  Good evening Nicole, I hope I'm not disturbing you.

NICOLE  Pierre! Good evening. I was just thinking of you.

PIERRE  You're not too busy?

NICOLE  No, no. I was writing a letter, when you knocked at the door.

PIERRE  Really? [literally 'oh good?']. Who were you writing to?

NICOLE  To the Duponts.

PIERRE  The Duponts? I don't know them.

NICOLE  Yes, you do! The Duponts are the people who used to live above us [literally 'above at our place'] in Paris, who used to travel a lot, and whose children were so noisy.

PIERRE  Oh yes. I didn't know them very well [literally 'I used not to know them very well']. By the way, how's your work going?

NICOLE  Not too well. If only I could work part time, that would suit me fine.

PIERRE  What would you do with [literally 'of'] all that free time?

NICOLE  I'd paint, I'd draw. Michel and I [literally 'Michel and I, we'] would go out more often, we'd go to the cinema, to restaurants. I'd do some sport, I'd learn English, I'd read all the books I bought last year, I …

PIERRE  The best thing for you would be to retire immediately! [Literally 'You would do better to take your retirement immediately.']

8

# Self-assessment test 2 A–C

This self-assessment test, based on weeks 5–8, will enable you to check on your progress and to see whether any revision is needed. Deduct one mark for every grammatical mistake or wrong spelling. The answers and score assessment are in the Key.

**A** Prepositions    Total: 8 marks

Complete the following:

1  Il y a un taxi [in front of] l'hôtel.
2  Il y a un restaurant [next to] la banque.
3  Il y a une librairie [opposite] l'université.
4  Il y a un tunnel [under] la Manche.
5  Est-ce qu'il y a une cabine téléphonique [near] la gare?
6  C'est difficile de travailler [without] ma secrétaire.
7  Nous pouvons manger [after] le spectacle.
8  Téléphonez [before] neuf heures.

**B** The perfect tense    Total: 10 marks

Imagine the following: You are a journalist (male or female). This morning you arrived at the hotel at seven o'clock. You went to an international conference at ten o'clock You left very late. Now complete these sentences:

1  Je suis j….
2  Ce m… je … … à l'hôtel à sept heures.
3  Je … … à une c… i … à dix heures.
4  Je … … très t….

**C** The weather  Total: 10 marks

Suggest the likely weather at the times and in the places indicated:

1  En Grande-Bretagne, au mois d'avril.
2  À Nice, au mois d'août.
3  À Londres, au mois de novembre.
4  En Russie, au mois de décembre.
5  En Écosse, en hiver.

8

**D** Countries    Total: 12 marks

Below are some simple clues to the names of countries. Identify the country and give its French name.

1  Son porto est très bon.
2  Le mont Fuji-Yama.
3  La statue de la Liberté.
4  La capitale? Athènes.
5  Cervantès.
6  Léonard de Vinci.
7  Ses tulipes sont belles.
8  La Révolution culturelle.
9  La capitale? Bruxelles.
10  Liberté, Egalité, Fraternité.
11  Shakespeare.
12  La capitale? Copenhague.

**E** Numbers    Total: 14 marks

Complete the following, writing the totals in words:

a  30 + 28
b  40 + 30
c  15 + 60
d  40 + 43
e  50 + 40
f  10 + 89
g  50 + 50

**F** The imperfect tense    Total: 14 marks

Talk about your French friends, Hélène and Pierre:

1  He used to play football.
2  She used to learn English.
3  They used to live in a large house.
4  They were doing the shopping when she lost her purse.

# Self-assessment test 2  G–I

**G** The conditional tense    Total: 8 marks

'If only …'. Answer the questions as indicated:

**1** Qu'est-ce que vous feriez, si vous étiez riche?
[visit Japan and China]

**2** Qu'est-ce que Monique ferait, si elle parlait italien?
[work as a bilingual secretary]

**3** Qu'est-ce que je ferais, si j'étais au chômage?
[look for work – use 'tu']

**4** Qu'est-ce que nous ferions, si nous avions
beaucoup de temps?
[read a great deal – use 'nous']

**H** Do you remember…?    Total: 4 marks

**a** What's the difference between the verbs 'savoir'
and 'connaître', both meaning 'to know'?

**b** What's the difference in meaning between 'je ne
sais pas jouer du piano' and 'je ne peux pas jouer
du piano'?

**I** Conversation (role-play)    Total: 20 marks
Play the part of Hélène in this dialogue:

HÉLÈNE   I've decided to change my life. I'm going to
watch television less often. I'll eat more
fruit. I'll do exercises each morning. I'll
spend less money on clothes.

MICHEL   Tu penses que tu seras plus heureuse?

HÉLÈNE   Yes, I'll have more time and more money,
and I'll be in better health.

8

# Week 9

- demonstrative pronouns ('this one', 'that one', 'these', 'those')
- possessive pronouns ('mine', 'yours', 'hers', etc)
- more question words and formations
- more about adverbs and adverbial expressions
- another quartet of irregular verbs

## 56 DEMONSTRATIVE PRONOUNS: THIS ONE, THAT ONE, THESE, THOSE

In English, a sentence like 'I prefer my doctor to the doctor who came this morning' would normally be shortened to 'I prefer my doctor to the one who came this morning'. In French, we express 'the one', 'those', as follows:

| | |
|---|---|
| **celui (m.)** | the one |
| **ceux (m. pl.)** | those |
| **celle (f.)** | the one |
| **celles (f. pl.)** | those |

Examples:

**Je préfère mon médecin à celui qui est venu ce matin.**
I prefer my doctor to the one who came this morning.
**Cette infirmière et celle qui a pris votre tension.**
This nurse and the one who took your blood pressure.
**J'ai apporté vos comprimés et ceux de votre mari.**
I've brought your tablets and your husband's (lit. 'those of your husband').

We would normally change 'this dentist and that dentist' to 'this dentist and that one'. In French, 'this one', 'that one', 'these', 'those' become:

| masculine | | feminine | |
|---|---|---|---|
| **celui-ci** | this one | **celle-ci** | this one |
| **celui-là** | that one | **celle-là** | that one |
| **ceux-ci** | these | **celles-ci** | these |
| **ceux-là** | those | **celles-là** | those |

Examples:
**Cet hôpital-ci ou celui-là?**
This hospital or that one?
**Quelle ambulance préférez-vous, celle-ci ou celle-là?**
Which ambulance do you prefer, this one or that one?
**Quels médicaments prenez-vous, ceux-ci ou ceux-là?**
Which medicines do you take, these or those?

If you prefer not to refer to an object by name but to call it simply 'this' or 'that', you can use the following words:

**ceci**          this
**cela** (or **ça**)    that

Examples:
**Je voudrais acheter ceci.**
I'd like to buy this.
**Le** (or **la**) **malade m'a donné cela.**
The patient gave me that.

'This', 'that', 'these', 'those', followed by the verb 'to be', are all normally translated by **c'est** or **ce sont**:

**C'est votre petit déjeuner, Monsieur.**
This is your breakfast, Sir.
**Ce sont** (or **c'est**) **les ordonnances que vous avez demandées.**
These are the prescriptions you asked for.

**C'est, ce sont** can also mean 'he/she is' and 'they are':

**C'est un dentiste** (or **Il est dentiste**). He's a dentist.

9

## Exercise 50

Translate:

1 My cold is worse than my sister's.
2 This hospital is more modern than the one the Princess visited last year.
3 Which surgeon carried out the heart transplant? This one or that one?
4 Have you an appointment with this dentist or that one?
5 The physiotherapist gave me this.
6 The chemist prepared that.
7 This is your new secretary.
8 These are your patients.

9

## 57 POSSESSIVE PRONOUNS: MINE, YOURS, HERS, ETC

Instead of saying 'The waiter has brought your soup but not my soup', we would usually say 'The waiter has brought your soup but not mine'. In French, the form of the possessive pronouns ('mine', 'yours', 'hers', etc) must reflect the gender and number of the noun they replace.

Pronouns replacing masculine nouns:

| singular | plural | |
|----------|--------|--|
| **le mien** | **les miens** | mine |
| **le tien** | **les tiens** | yours (fam.) |
| **le sien** | **les siens** | his/hers |
| **le nôtre** | **les nôtres** | ours |
| **le vôtre** | **les vôtres** | yours |
| **le leur** | **les leurs** | theirs |

Pronouns replacing feminine nouns:

| | | |
|--|--|--|
| **la mienne** | **les miennes** | mine |
| **la tienne** | **les tiennes** | yours (fam.) |
| **la sienne** | **les siennes** | his/hers |
| **la nôtre** | **les nôtres** | ours |
| **la vôtre** | **les vôtres** | yours |
| **la leur** | **les leurs** | theirs |

Examples:

**Le garçon a apporté votre soupe, mais pas la mienne.**
The waiter has brought your soup, but not mine.

**Voici son croissant, mais où est le vôtre?**
Here's his/her croissant, but where's yours?

**Notre jambon est très bon; comment est le leur?**
Our ham is very good; how's theirs?

**Ma bière est excellente; est-ce que la vôtre est bonne aussi?**
My beer is excellent; is yours good too?

**J'ai payé mon café, mais je n'ai pas payé les leurs.**
I've paid for my coffee, but I haven't paid for theirs.

9

When following the verb 'to be' and having the meaning of 'belonging to', the possessive pronouns are often translated by:

| | |
|---|---|
| **à moi** | **à nous** |
| **à toi** | **à vous** |
| **à lui** | **à eux (m. pl.)** |
| **à elle** | **à elles (f. pl.)** |

It is also possible to say **à Pierre**, **à ma femme**, etc, meaning 'Pierre's', 'my wife's':

**Pardon, Madame, est-ce que ce parapluie est à vous?**
Excuse me, Madam, is this umbrella yours?
**Ces gants (m.) ne sont pas à moi; ils sont à mon frère.**
These gloves are not mine; they belong to my brother.

## 58 MORE QUESTION FORMS

**1** 'What ...?' is expressed as follows:

After a preposition, by **quoi**:

**À quoi pensez-vous?**
What are you thinking about?
**Je pense à mon déjeuner.**
I'm thinking about my lunch.
**Avec quoi avez-vous payé le dîner?**
What did you pay for the dinner with?
**J'ai payé avec ma carte de crédit.**
I paid with my credit card.

Before the verb 'to be' and a noun, by **quel, quelle, quels, quelles**:

**Quel est votre nom?**
What is your name?
**Quel est votre numéro de téléphone?**
What is your telephone number?

9

**Quelle est votre adresse?**
What is your address?
**Quels sont les prix?**
What are the prices?

When subject of the sentence, by **qu'est-ce qui**:

**Délicieux? Qu'est-ce qui est délicieux?**
Delicious? What's delicious?

When object of the sentence, by **qu'est-ce que**
or **que (qu')**:

**Qu'est-ce que vous avez comme légumes?**
or **Qu'avez-vous comme légumes?**
What have you got in the way of vegetables?

As an exclamation, 'What!' is translated by **Quoi!**:

**Quoi! Le service n'est pas compris?**
What! The service isn't included ?
**Quoi! Le bar est fermé?**
What! The bar is closed?
**Quoi! Le café n'est pas ouvert?**
What! The cafe isn't open?

As an exclamation, 'what' followed by a noun is
translated by **quel, quelle, quels, quelles**:

**Quel repas! Quelle cuisinière!**
What a meal! What a cook!

**2** 'Who, Whom ...?' is expressed as follows:

When subject of the sentence, by **qui** or **qui est-ce qui**:

**Qui est-ce qui a réservé la table?**
Who reserved the table?

When object of the sentence, by **qui** or **qui est-ce que**:

**9**

**Qui est-ce que vous avez payé? La serveuse?**
Whom did you pay? The waitress?
**Avec qui avez-vous mangé?**
Who(m.) did you eat with?

**3** 'Which one(s) …?' is expressed by **lequel, laquelle, lesquels, lesquelles**:

**Voici trois bons vins. À votre avis, lequel est le meilleur?**
Here are three good wines. In your opinion, which one is the best?
**Toutes les tables sont libres, Madame; laquelle préférez-vous?**
All the tables are free, Madam; which one do you prefer?
**Des légumes? Oui, lesquels voulez-vous?**
Vegetables? Yes, which would you like?

**4** We saw in section 15 that 'Which book?', 'Which house?', etc, are translated as **Quel livre?**, **Quelle maison?** etc. For example:

**Quel vin avez-vous bu?** Which wine did you drink?

Note that where, as in the last example, **quel** appears in a sentence with a perfect tense verb using **avoir**, the past participle must agree with it in gender and number:

**Quelle viande avez-vous mangée?**
Which meat did you eat?
**Quels plats avez-vous recommandés?**
Which dishes did you recommend?
**Quelles pommes avez-vous achetées?**
Which apples did you buy?

This does not apply if **quel** is preceded by a preposition:

**À quelle femme avez-vous donné le livre?**
Which woman did you give the book to?

**5** 'Whose …?' is translated by **à qui**:

**À qui est ce dessert?** Whose is this dessert?
**À qui est cette serviette?** Whose is this napkin?

## VOCABULARY

| | |
|---|---|
| **le barman** | barman |
| **le whisky** | whisky |
| **le poisson** | fish |
| **le repas** | meal |
| **le couteau** | knife |
| **le chapeau** | hat |
| **la fourchette** | fork |
| **la cuillère** | spoon |
| **les baguettes (f.)** | chopsticks |
| **frais, fraîche (f.)** | fresh |
| **chinois** | Chinese |
| **italien** | Italian |
| **commander** | to order |

## IRREGULAR VERBS

**sentir** (to smell)      **servir** (to serve)

Present tense            Present tense
**je sens**               **je sers**
**tu sens**               **tu sers**
**il/elle sent**          **il/elle sert**
**nous sentons**          **nous servons**
**vous sentez**           **vous servez**
**ils/elles sentent**     **ils/elles servent**

**partir** (to leave)

Present tense
**je pars**
**tu pars**
**il/elle part**
**nous partons**
**vous partez**
**ils/elles partent**

9

NOTE: **payer** (to pay) is not irregular, but is one of those verbs which change their spelling in the stem (see section 81). As seen in the following present tense, **y** becomes **i** before a silent **e**.

| | |
|---|---|
| **je paie** | **nous payons** |
| **tu paies** | **vous payez** |
| **il/elle paie** | **ils/elles paient** |

## Exercise 51

Translate:

1 The barman has served you your whisky, but where's mine?
2 My fish is delicious; yours is not fresh.
3 I've paid our bill and they've paid theirs.
4 Does this hat belong to you or to your friend (m.)?
5 What do you want to eat this Chinese meal with? With chopsticks? What! No! With a knife and fork.
6 What is the telephone number of the Italian restaurant?
7 Which vegetables did she order?
8 What smells so good?
9 Here's a list of the best restaurants in Paris; which one do you prefer?
10 Whose is this spoon?

**9**

## 59 MORE ADVERBS

We can form adverbs from adjectives ending in **-ant**, **-ent** by changing the **-nt** to **-mment**:

**constant** becomes **constamment** 'constantly'
**évident** becomes **évidemment** 'obviously'

Note: an important exception is **lent, lentement** 'slowly'.

A few adjectives can be used as adverbs without any change:

**La soupe sent bon.** The soup smells good.
**Le poisson sent mauvais.** The fish smells bad.
**Frappez fort.** Knock loudly.
**Parlez plus bas.** Speak more softly.

Here is a list of useful adverbs and adverbial expressions (see also section 31):

Time

| | |
|---|---|
| **tôt** | early |
| **tard** | late |
| **maintenant** | now |
| **tout de suite** | immediately |
| **immédiatement** | immediately |
| **ensuite** | afterwards |
| **toujours** | always, still |
| **hier** | yesterday |
| **aujourd'hui** | today |
| **demain** | tomorrow |
| **ce matin** | this morning |
| **cet après-midi** | this afternoon |
| **ce soir** | this evening |
| **souvent** | often |
| **rarement** | rarely |

Place

| | |
|---|---|
| **ici** | here |
| **là** | here, there |
| **là-bas** | over there |
| **à droite** | on/to the right |
| **à gauche** | on/to the left |
| **en haut** | upstairs |
| **en bas** | downstairs |
| **partout** | everywhere |

Certainty

| | |
|---|---|
| **sûrement** | certainly, surely |
| **certainement** | certainly |

9

Doubt

| | |
|---|---|
| **peut-être** | perhaps |
| **probablement** | probably |

Manner

| | |
|---|---|
| **bien** | well |
| **mal** | badly |
| **ensemble** | together |
| **surtout** | especially |
| **exprès** | on purpose |
| **vite** | quickly |
| **rapidement** | rapidly |
| **lentement** | slowly |
| **déjà** | already |
| **encore** | still, yet |

## 60 POSITION OF ADVERBS

In French, adverbs are placed after the verb, never between the subject and verb, as in English:

**Il parle rarement anglais.**
He rarely speaks English.
**Elle va souvent au théâtre.**
She often goes to the theatre.

In compound tenses (e.g. the perfect tense) the following adverbs are normally placed between **avoir** (or **être**) and the past participle:

| | |
|---|---|
| **bien** | **toujours** |
| **mal** | **souvent** |
| **vite** | **beaucoup** |
| **encore** | **déjà** |

Examples:
**Vous avez bien répondu à la question.**
You have answered the question well.
**Je n'ai pas encore lu votre lettre.**
I haven't read your letter yet.

**Votre frère est déjà parti?**
Has your brother already left?

But when the adverb is an important word in the sentence, it generally comes at the end:

**Je vais écrire la lettre maintenant.**
I'm going to write the letter now.

## VOCABULARY

| | |
|---|---|
| **le bain** | bath |
| **neiger** | to snow |
| **pleuvoir** | to rain |

## Exercise 52

Give the opposite of:

1 Ils chantent bien.
2 Ne parlez pas si fort.
3 Il va rarement chez ses parents.
4 Nous n'avons pas encore mangé.
5 Il va peut-être pleuvoir ou neiger.
6 Elle prend un bain en haut.
7 Elles feront les courses demain.

9

## VOCABULARY

| | |
|---|---|
| **le mariage** | wedding, marriage |
| **le mannequin** | model, dummy |
| **la veste** | jacket |
| **la taille** | size |
| **la couleur** | colour |
| **la mode** | fashion |
| **la laine** | wool |
| **la vitrine** | shop window |
| **la vente** | sale |
| **bleu marine** | navy blue |
| **gris clair** | light grey |
| **pur** | pure |
| **court** | short |
| **long, longue (f.)** | long |
| **(mal)heureusement** | (un)fortunately |
| **exactement** | exactly |
| **être en train de** | to be in the middle of (doing something) |
| **essayer** | to try, to try on |
| **ne ... que** | only |

## IRREGULAR VERB

**plaire** (to please)

Present tense
**je plais**
**tu plais**
**il/elle plaît**
**nous plaisons**
**vous plaisez**
**ils/elles plaisent**

Perfect tense
**j'ai plu**, etc

*Une veste à la mode*

CLIENT    **Bonjour, Madame. Je vais à un mariage la semaine prochaine … heureusement pas le mien … et je voudrais acheter une veste … une veste très chic.**

VENDEUSE    **Oui, quelle est votre taille, Monsieur?**

CLIENT    **Je fais du 42.**

VENDEUSE    **Quelle couleur préférez-vous?**

CLIENT    **Je veux surtout une couleur à la mode.**

VENDEUSE    **Eh bien, j'ai cette veste-ci en bleu marine en pure laine, et celle-là en gris clair.**

CLIENT    **Hm, j'aurais préféré une veste comme celle que vous avez en vitrine. Elle me plaît beaucoup.**

VENDEUSE    **Malheureusement, je n'ai plus votre taille, Monsieur. Je n'ai que des petites tailles.**

CLIENT    **Et celle sur le mannequin, ici dans le magasin?**

VENDEUSE    **C'est aussi une petite taille. Je pense qu'elle sera trop courte pour vous.**

CLIENT    **Mais … regardez! Regardez celle-là! C'est exactement ce qu'il me faut. Je vais l'essayer tout de suite.**

VENDEUSE    **Non, non, non, Monsieur! Cette veste-là n'est pas en vente. Elle est à ce monsieur là-bas qui est en train d'essayer un costume!**

**9**

*A fashionable jacket*

| | |
|---|---|
| CUSTOMER | Good morning. I'm going to a wedding next week ... fortunately not mine ... and I'd like to buy a jacket ... a fashionable jacket. |
| SALES ASSISTANT | Yes, what is your size, Sir? |
| CUSTOMER | I take size 42 [literally 'I do some 42']. |
| SALES ASSISTANT | What colour do you prefer? |
| CUSTOMER | I particularly want a colour that's in fashion. |
| SALES ASSISTANT | Well, I have this jacket in navy blue in pure wool, and that one in light grey. |
| CUSTOMER | Hm, I would have preferred a jacket like the one you have in the window. I like it very much [literally 'It pleases me much']. |
| SALES ASSISTANT | Unfortunately, I no longer have your size, Sir. I have only small sizes. |
| CUSTOMER | What about [literally 'And'] the one which is on the model, here in the shop? |
| SALES ASSISTANT | That's also a small size. I think it will be too short for you. |
| CUSTOMER | But ... look! Look at that one! That's exactly what I need. I'm going to try it on right away. |
| SALES ASSISTANT | No, no, no, Sir, that jacket is not for sale! It belongs to that gentleman over there who's trying on a suit! |

9

# Week 10

- *reflexive verbs ('se laver', 'to wash oneself', as distinct from 'laver', 'to wash')*
- *verbs preceded by prepositions*
- *the translation of 'to' before an infinitive*
- *the order of pronouns*
- *the pronouns 'en', 'y', 'on'*

## 61 REFLEXIVE VERBS ('SE LAVER')

Study the following:

| laver | to wash | se laver | to wash oneself |
|-------|---------|----------|-----------------|
| raser | to shave | se raser | to shave oneself |
| brûler | to burn | se brûler | to burn oneself |
| perdre | to lose | se perdre | to lose oneself |
| couper | to cut | se couper | to cut oneself |
| préparer | to prepare | se préparer | to prepare oneself |
| amuser | to amuse | s'amuser | to enjoy oneself |
| habiller | to dress | s'habiller | to dress oneself |

The verbs in the second column are being used reflexively. The present tense of a reflexive verb goes like this:

Present tense

| je me lave | I wash myself |
|------------|---------------|
| tu te rases | you (fam.) shave yourself |
| il se brûle | he burns himself |
| elle se prépare | she prepares herself |
| nous nous amusons | we enjoy ourselves |
| vous vous habillez | you dress yourself (yourselves) |
| ils se perdent | they (m.) lose themselves |
| elles se coupent | they (f.) cut themselves |

Note: **me**, **te**, and **se** become **m'**, **t'**, and **s'** before a vowel or h.

All reflexive verbs use **être** to form the perfect tense. The past participle agrees in gender and number with the person or persons performing the reflexive action:

10

Perfect tense

| | |
|---|---|
| **je me suis lavé(e)** | I washed myself |
| **tu t'es habillé(e)** | you (fam.) dressed yourself |
| **il s'est rasé** | he shaved himself |
| **elle ne s'est pas amusée** | she did not enjoy herself |
| **nous nous sommes préparé(e)s** | we prepared ourselves |
| **vous ne vous êtes pas perdu(e)** | you didn't lose yourself |
| **vous ne vous êtes pas perdu(e)s** | you didn't lose yourselves |
| **ils se sont brûlés** | they burnt themselves |
| **elles ne se sont pas coupées** | they didn't cut themselves |

Imperfect tense

| | |
|---|---|
| **je me lavais** | I used to wash or I was washing myself |

Future tense

| | |
|---|---|
| **je me laverai** | I will wash myself |

Conditional tense

| | |
|---|---|
| **je me laverais** | I would wash myself |

Note that in English we don't always add the reflexive pronoun, but say simply 'I wash', 'he shaves'. In French the reflexive pronoun must always be used. Compare:

| | |
|---|---|
| **Je me rase.** | I shave. |
| **Je rase mon père.** | I shave my father. |

Reflexive verbs are much more common in French than in English. Here is a list for reference:

| | |
|---|---|
| **se déshabiller** | to undress |
| **s'endormir** | to fall asleep |
| **se réveiller** | to wake up |
| **se lever** | to get up |
| **se dépêcher** | to hurry |
| **se promener** | to go for a walk |

10

| | |
|---|---|
| **se reposer** | to rest |
| **se coucher** | to go to bed |
| **se tromper** | to make a mistake |
| **s'appeler** | to be called |
| **se marier** | to get married |
| **se débarrasser de** | to get rid of |
| **se servir de** | to make use of |
| **se souvenir de** | to remember |

It is important to distinguish between 'myself', 'yourself', etc used reflexively and the same words used for emphasis. Compare:

**Je me lave.**
I wash myself.
**Je lave les enfants moi-même.**
I wash the children myself.

The '-self' words used emphatically are:

| | |
|---|---|
| **moi-même** | **nous-mêmes** |
| **toi-même** | **vous-même(s)** |
| **lui-même** | **eux-mêmes** |
| **elle-même** | **elles-mêmes** |

## VOCABULARY

| | |
|---|---|
| **se peigner** | to comb one's hair |
| **se maquiller** | to put on one's make-up |
| **se laver les mains (f.)** | to wash one's hands |
| **se brosser les dents (f.)** | to brush one's teeth |

10

## Exercise 53

This is what Paul does each day.
Translate:

1 He wakes up at 7 a.m.
2 He washes.
3 He shaves.
4 He goes to work.

And now Monique:

5 She gets up at 8 a.m.
6 She takes a shower.
7 She combs her hair.
8 She puts her make-up on.
9 She goes to the station.

This is what you and I do:

10 We wash.
11 We dress quickly.
12 We go for a walk.
13 We go to bed at 10 p.m.

Translate:

14 I (f.) have enjoyed myself.
15 You (f.) have not made a mistake.
16 They (f.) are resting.
17 They (m.) have washed the car themselves.
18 We brush our teeth each morning.

10

Reflexive pronouns are used in sentences where in English we use 'one another' or 'each other':

**Nous nous sommes souvent rencontrés.**
We often met (one another).
**Les Américains et les Chinois ne se comprennent pas.**
The Americans and the Chinese don't understand each other.

Note: In the perfect tense the past participle of the verb (**téléphoné**) does not agree with **me**, **se**, etc when the meaning is 'to or for myself, himself, etc'. Compare:

**Ils se sont rencontrés.** They met each other.
**Ils se sont téléphoné.** They telephoned (to) each other.

## 62 VERBS PRECEDED BY PREPOSITIONS

Study the following:

1 I'm used to *getting up* very early.
2 He left *without saying* goodbye.
3 She hesitated *before replying*.
4 *After buying* a computer, he worked much more quickly.
5 These CDs are excellent *for improving* one's pronunciation.
6 He began *by criticising* the managing director.

You will notice that, in English, verbs preceded by a preposition end in -ing. In French, the infinitive is used:

1 **Je suis habitué à me lever très tôt.**
2 **Il est parti sans dire au revoir.**
3 **Elle a hésité avant de répondre.**
4 **Après avoir acheté un ordinateur, il a travaillé beaucoup plus vite.**
5 **Ces CD sont excellents pour améliorer sa prononciation.**
6 **Il a commencé par critiquer le président-directeur général.**

10

There is one exception to the above rule, namely the preposition **en**, which is followed by the present participle. This will be dealt with in section 71.

Note also that, although the English is usually 'after buying' etc, the French has to be 'after having bought', **après avoir acheté** or, in the case of those verbs that instead use **être**, **après être** ....

## VOCABULARY

| | |
|---|---|
| **le mot** | word |
| **le ménage** | housework |
| **l'électricien (m.)** | electrician |
| **la lampe** | lamp |
| **partir** | to leave |
| **quitter** | to leave (with object) |
| **tout le monde** | everyone |

## Exercise 54

Translate:

1 He left the house without saying a word.
2 She's used to listening to the radio in her bedroom.
3 Before repairing the lamp, he telephoned the electrician.
4 After preparing breakfast, he did the housework.
5 My mother began by saying that the family was in good health and finished by wishing everyone a happy New Year.
6 These CDs are excellent for learning French.

10

## 63 TRANSLATION OF 'TO' BEFORE AN INFINITIVE

Compare the following French and English sentences:

**1 Je dois apprendre le français.**
I have to learn French.
**2 J'ai décidé d'apprendre le français.**
I have decided to learn French.
**3 J'ai commencé à apprendre le français.**
I have started to learn French.
**4 J'ai acheté ce livre pour apprendre le français.**
I have bought this book to learn French.

You will see from the above sentences that 'to' coming before an infinitive is sometimes:

**1** not translated
**2** translated by **de (d')**
**3** translated by **à**
**4** translated by **pour**

Unfortunately, there is only one rule to help us decide which preposition to use and it's this: when 'to' means 'in order to', use **pour**.

The rest of the time it's simply a question of learning by heart which verbs take no preposition, which take **de** and which take **à**.

Here are some lists for reference, followed by a few model sentences as examples.

'To' is not translated before an infinitive after these verbs:

| | |
|---|---|
| **aimer** | to like, to love |
| **préférer** | to prefer |
| **vouloir** | to want |
| **désirer** | to wish |
| **aller** | to go |
| **venir** | to come |

| devoir | to have to |
|---|---|
| **falloir (il faut)** | to be necessary |
| **espérer** | to hope |
| **pouvoir** | to be able |
| **savoir** | to know how |

'To' is translated by **de** before an infinitive after these verbs:

| cesser | to stop |
|---|---|
| **conseiller** | to advise |
| **décider** | to decide |
| **demander** | to ask |
| **dire** | to tell |
| **empêcher** | to prevent |
| **essayer** | to try to avoid |
| **éviter** | to finish |
| **finir** | to finish |
| **oublier** | to forget |
| **permettre** | to allow |
| **persuader** | to persuade |
| **promettre** | to promise |
| **proposer** | to propose |
| **refuser** | to refuse |
| **regretter** | to regret |

Note also:

| être content de | to be pleased to |
|---|---|
| **être heureux de** | to be happy to |
| **être ravi de** | to be delighted to |
| **être triste de** | to be sad to |
| **être désolé de** | to be sorry to |
| **avoir l'intention de** | to intend to |
| **avoir l'occasion de** | to have the opportunity to |
| **avoir le temps de** | to have the time to |
| **avoir le plaisir de** | to have the pleasure to |
| **il est facile de** | it is easy to |
| **il est difficile de** | it is difficult to |
| **il est possible de** | it is possible to |
| **il est impossible de** | it is impossible to |
| **il est permis de** | it is permitted to |

| | |
|---|---|
| **il est défendu de** | it is forbidden to |
| **il est temps de** | it is time to |

'To' is translated by **à** before an infinitive coming after these verbs:

| | |
|---|---|
| **aider** | to help |
| **apprendre** | to learn |
| **avoir** | to have |
| **commencer** | to begin |
| **continuer** | to continue |
| **encourager** | to encourage |
| **enseigner** | to teach |
| **hésiter** | to hesitate |
| **inviter** | to invite |
| **réussir** | to succeed |

Note also:

| | |
|---|---|
| **être prêt à** | to be ready to |
| **être disposé à** | to be willing to |
| **avoir de la difficulté à** | to have difficulty in |
| **avoir du mal à** | to have difficulty in |

Examples:
**Je préfère aller me baigner.**
I prefer to go for a swim.
**Nous espérons aller à la plage cet après-midi.**
We hope to go to the beach this afternoon.
**Ils ont décidé de louer un pédalo.**
They have decided to hire a pedal boat.
**Je vous conseille de faire une promenade en bateau.**
I advise you to go on a boat trip.
**Nous sommes contents de voir le soleil.**
We are pleased to see the sun .
**Avez-vous réussi à trouver des chaises longues?**
Did you succeed in finding some deckchairs?
**Nous l'avons aidée à chercher des coquillages (m.).**
We helped her to look for some shells.
**Il est temps de rentrer à l'hôtel.**
It's time to return to the hotel.

10

## Exercise 55

Complete the following:

1 (I intend to) acheter des lunettes de soleil.
2 (Will it be possible to) faire des excursions?
3 (We prefer to) louer un appartement.
4 (They (m.) invited me (f.) to) aller à la pêche.
5 (I hesitate to) faire du ski nautique.
6 (Will you have the opportunity to) faire de la planche à voile?

## 64 ORDER OF PRONOUNS ('HE GAVE IT TO ME')

In sentences such as 'he gave it to him' or 'I'm sending them to you', French uses a different word order from English. Notice that **le**, **la**, **l'**, **les** follow **me**, **vous**, **nous**:

**Paul me le donne.** Paul gives it to me.
**Nicole nous la vend.** Nicole sells it to us.
**Je vous les enverrai.** I'll send them to you.

But **le**, **la**, **l'**, **les** precede **lui** and **leur**:

**Nous le lui avons déjà montré.**
We have already shown it to him (or to her).
**Vous la leur avez donnée?**
Did you give it to them?
**Je ne les lui ai pas vendus.**
I didn't sell them to him (or to her).

## VOCABULARY

| | |
|---|---|
| **le dossier** | file |
| **le/la collègue** | colleague |
| **le fax** | fax |
| **la moto** | motorbike |
| **la facture** | invoice |

## Exercise 56

Replace all nouns with pronouns (and make any necessary changes):

1 Est-ce que vous m'avez donné le dossier?
2 Notre directeur nous a promis les deux voitures.
3 Mon collègue a l'intention de me vendre ses livres.
4 J'ai envoyé un fax à Paul.
5 Pierre montre sa nouvelle moto à Monique.
6 Nous avons donné les factures aux clients.

10

**En** replaces a word or an idea introduced by **de**.
**En** means:

**1** 'Some' or 'any', when not followed by a noun:

**Avez-vous des journaux américains?**
Do you have any English newspapers?
**Oui, nous en avons.**
Yes, we have some.
**Non, nous n'en avons pas.**
No, we don't have any.

Note that 'some', 'any' must be expressed in French,
even if omitted in English:

**Avez-vous des enveloppes (f.)?** Do you have any
envelopes?
**Oui, j'en ai.** Yes, I have.

**2** 'Of it', 'of them':

**Avez-vous acheté de l'essence (f.)?**
Did you buy any petrol?
**Oui, j'en ai acheté beaucoup.**
Yes, I bought a lot (of it).
**Ont-ils des enfants?**
Do they have any children?
**Oui, ils en ont deux.**
Yes, they have two (of them).

**3** 'About it', 'about them':

**Avez-vous parlé de la navette spatiale?**
Did you talk about (of) the space shuttle?
**Oui, tous les astronautes en parlent!**
Yes, all the astronauts are talking about it!

**4** 'From there':

**Est-ce que les ingénieurs vont au centre de contrôle?**
Are the engineers going to the control centre?
**Non, ils en viennent.**
No, they've just come (lit. 'they come') from there.

## 66 USEFUL PRONOUNS: 'Y'

**Y** replaces a word or an idea introduced by **à**. **Y** means:

**1** 'There':

**Est-ce que Paul connaît les Etats-Unis?**
Does Paul know the United States?
**Oui, il y a passé trois ans.**
Yes, he spent three years there.
**Est-ce que tu viens de la gare?**
Are you (fam.) coming from the station?
**Non, j'y vais.**
No, I'm going there.

Note: when actually pointing, use **là** or **là-bas** for 'there'.

**2** 'To it', 'to them':

**Il faut toujours faire la queue à Moscou.**
One always has to queue in Moscow.
**Oui, mais les Russes y sont habitués.**
Yes, but the Russians are used to it.

Note that **y** cannot be omitted:

**Est-ce que le directeur est dans son bureau?**
Is the director in his office?
**Oui, il y est.**
Yes, he is.

10

## 67 USEFUL PRONOUNS: 'ON'

In English, when referring to people in general, we use words such as 'one', 'they', 'you', 'people', e.g. 'In England people drive on the left' or 'In China they eat with chopsticks'. In sentences like these the French use the pronoun **on**, followed by the same form of the verb as with **il** or **elle**:

**En Angleterre on roule à gauche.**
In England they drive on the left.
**En Chine on mange avec des baguettes.**
In China they eat with chopsticks.
**On dit qu'il parle sept langues.**
People say he speaks seven languages.

**On** is often used to translate the English passive:

**On a invité les diplomates chinois à l'Ambassade de France.**
The Chinese diplomats have been invited to the French Embassy.

Informally in conversation, the French often use **on** in place of **nous**:

**Alors, on va partir aujourd'hui ou demain?**
Well, are we going to leave today or tomorrow?

Note: **on** sometimes becomes **l'on** after **et** and **si**; the French find this sound more pleasant to the ear.

10

## VOCABULARY

| | |
|---|---|
| le banc | bench |
| l'attitude | attitude |
| la promotion | promotion |
| la chance | luck |
| la platine laser | CD player |
| sociable | sociable |
| récemment | recently |
| encore | again |
| bien sûr | of course |
| alors | well |
| lorsque | when |
| perfectionner | to perfect |
| apprécier | to appreciate |
| s'acheter | to buy for oneself |

## IRREGULAR VERBS

**s'asseoir** (to sit down)

Present tense
**je m'assieds**
**tu t'assieds**
**il/elle s'assied**
**nous nous asseyons**
**vous vous asseyez**
**ils/elles s'asseyent**

Perfect tense
**je me suis assis**, etc

Future tense
**je m'assiérai**, etc

**obtenir** (to obtain, to get)

Present tense
**j'obtiens**
**tu obtiens**
**il/elle obtient**
**nous obtenons**
**vous obtenez**
**ils/elles obtiennent**

Perfect tense
**j'ai obtenu**, etc

Future tense
**j'obtiendrai**, etc

**sortir** (to go out)

Present tense
**je sors**
**tu sors**
**il/elle sort**

**nous sortons**
**vous sortez**
**ils/elles sortent**

10

*L'anglais en trois mois*

DAVID  Est-ce que vous vous servez toujours de la platine laser que vous avez achetée récemment?

ISABELLE  Non, je ne me sers plus de celle-là. Je m'en suis débarrassée et je me suis acheté un baladeur beaucoup plus perfectionné.

DAVID  N'est-il pas difficile d'apprécier la musique avec une si petite machine?

ISABELLE  Vous vous trompez, ce n'est pas de la musique que j'écoute, ce sont des CD d'anglais. Je les ai achetés parce que je dois apprendre l'anglais en trois mois.

DAVID  Est-ce que vous avez le temps d'écouter ces CD?

ISABELLE  Oui, bien sûr. Je les écoute le matin lorsque je me lave, lorsque je m'habille, lorsque je me peigne, lorsque je me maquille ... ce qui prend un certain temps. Mon mari écoute les CD aussi quand il se rase, quand il se lave et se brosse les dents. Le dimanche nous aimons sortir et j'écoute encore mes CD lorsque nous nous promenons au parc et lorsque nous nous asseyons sur un banc pour nous reposer.

DAVID  Ce n'est pas une attitude très sociable.

ISABELLE  C'est vrai, mais si je réussis à apprendre l'anglais en trois mois, il me sera possible d'obtenir une promotion et de voyager en Angleterre et aux États-Unis.

DAVID  Bon, alors, bonne chance ou comme on dit en anglais 'good luck'!

**10**

*English in three months*

DAVID   Are you still using the CD player you bought recently?

ISABELLE   No, I'm not using that one any more. I've got rid of it and I've bought myself a much more sophisticated [literally 'perfected'] personal stereo.

DAVID   Isn't it difficult to appreciate music with such a small machine?

ISABELLE   You're mistaken, it's not music I listen to, it's English-language CDs [literally 'CDs of English']. I bought them because I have to learn English in three months.

DAVID   Do you have the time to listen to these CDs?

ISABELLE   Yes, of course. I listen to them in the morning when I'm washing, when I'm getting dressed, when I'm combing my hair, when I'm putting my make-up on … which takes a while [literally 'a certain time']. My husband also listens to the CDs when he's shaving, when he's washing and brushing his teeth. On Sundays we like to go out and I listen to my CDs again when we're walking in the park and when we sit down on a bench for a rest.

DAVID   That's not a very sociable attitude.

ISABELLE   That's true, but if I succeed in learning English in three months, it will be possible for me to get promotion and to travel to England and the United States.

DAVID   Good, well, good luck or, as they say in English, 'good luck'!

**10**

# Week 11

- *conjunctions: words like 'because' and 'while', which join parts of a sentence together*
- *numbers over 100*
- *the passive voice*
- *the present participle*
- *more about the imperative form*
- *the pluperfect ('I had spoken', etc)*
- *using 'depuis' ('since') and 'venir de' ('to have just …')*

## 68 CONJUNCTIONS: BUT, BECAUSE, WHILE, ETC

Study the following:

Reason

| | |
|---|---|
| **parce que** | because |
| **car** | for, because |
| **puisque** | since |
| **comme** | as, since |
| **donc** | so, therefore |

Time

| | |
|---|---|
| **quand** | when |
| **lorsque** | when |
| **dès que** | as soon as |
| **aussitôt que** | as soon as |
| **pendant que** | while |
| **maintenant que** | now that |

Contrast

| | |
|---|---|
| **mais** | but |
| **tandis que** | whereas |

Examples:

**Nous avons acheté une tente, car nous voulons faire du camping.**
We have bought a tent, because we want to go camping.

11

**Mon père n'aime pas l'Italie, donc nous sommes allés en Allemagne.**
My father doesn't like Italy, so we went to Germany.
**Puisque tu es fatigué, nous pourrions camper ici.**
Since you're tired, we could camp here.
**Pendant que tu vas chercher de la bière, je vais regarder la télévision.**
While you go and get some beer, I'll watch television.
**C'est un bon camping, mais où sont les toilettes?**
It's a good campsite, but where are the toilets?

Note that you must use the future tense after **quand**, **lorsque**, **dès que**, and **aussitôt que** when the future is referred to:

**Quand nous ferons du camping l'année prochaine, toute la famille s'amusera bien.**
When we go camping next year, the whole family will have a good time.
**Aussitôt que tu seras prêt, je préparerai à manger.**
As soon as you're ready, I'll prepare something to eat.

BUT not if 'when' means 'whenever':

**Quand je suis en vacances, je dépense toujours beaucoup d'argent.**
When I'm on holiday, I always spend a lot of money.

## VOCABULARY

| | |
|---|---|
| **le sac de couchage** | sleeping bag |
| **le champ** | field |
| **la piscine** | swimming pool |
| **supplémentaire** | extra |
| **tomber en panne** | to break down |

**11**

## Exercise 57

Translate:

1 As Paul's friend (m.) is coming camping with us, we'll have to buy an extra sleeping bag.

2 When you can speak French, we'll go camping in France.

3 Do you take every opportunity to speak French, when you're in Belgium?

4 I don't like this campsite because there's no swimming pool.

5 There are four of us (say 'We are four') but we have only three sleeping bags.

6 The car broke down, so we decided to camp in a field.

## 69 NUMBERS OVER 100

Look at these numbers between a hundred and a million:

|  |  |
|---|---|
| 100 | cent |
| 101 | cent un |
| 110 | cent dix |
| 150 | cent cinquante |
| 200 | deux cents |
| 300 | trois cents |
| 400 | quatre cents |
| 520 | cinq cent vingt |
| 640 | six cent quarante |
| 750 | sept cent cinquante |
| 800 | huit cents |
| 960 | neuf cent soixante |
| 1000 | mille |
| 1250 | mille deux cent cinquante |
| 2000 | deux mille |
| 8000 | huit mille |
| 9000 | neuf mille |
| 1,000,000 | un million |

NOTE
**cent** drops the **s** when followed by another number:
**trois cents livres** BUT **trois cent quarante livres**

when followed by a noun, **un million** takes **de**:
**un million de francs**

in dates **mille** is sometimes written **mil**:
**en mille (or mil) neuf cent quatre-vingt-seize**
Ordinal numbers (first, second, etc) are formed like this:

| | | | |
|---|---|---|---|
| 1st | premier | 8th | huitième |
| 2nd | deuxième | 9th | neuvième |
| 3rd | troisième | 10th | dixième |
| 4th | quatrième | 20th | vingtième |
| 5th | cinquième | 21st | vingt et unième |
| 6th | sixième | 22nd | vingt-deuxième |
| 7th | septième | | |

NOTE
**premier** has a feminine form: **première**

**deuxième** has an alternative: **second, seconde (f.)**

the spelling of **cinquième** and **neuvième**

in French we don't say 'Louis the Fourteenth', we say
'Louis fourteen', etc: **Louis quatorze, Henri huit**

## Exercise 58

Complete the following, writing the answers in full:

**A** 150 + 100 =     **D** 450 + 120 =

**B** 260 + 40 =     **E** 580 + 100 =

**C** 320 + 110 =     **F** 1000 + 440 =

**11**

## Exercise 59

Translate:

1 the first disco
2 the second casino
3 the third night club
4 the fourth theatre
5 the fifth concert
6 the sixth opera
7 the seventh cinema
8 the eighth skating rink
9 the ninth ballet
10 the tenth restaurant

## 70 THE PASSIVE

The passive is formed as in English with the verb 'to be', **être**, and the past participle, e.g. **fait** (done). The past participle agrees with the subject; by is translated by **par**:

**Un tunnel sera construit l'année prochaine.**
A tunnel will be built next year.
**Le traité a été signé par les deux gouvernements.**
The treaty has been signed by both governments.

**11**

'By' is usually **par**, but may also be **de**, especially after verbs of feeling. Note also that the past participle changes to reflect the gender and number of the subject of the sentence:

**La Reine est respectée de tout le monde.**
The Queen is respected by everyone.

The French have a tendency to avoid the passive and do so in one of the following ways:

**1** By using the pronoun **on** (see week 10, section 67):

**On a déjà oublié le tunnel que les Britanniques ont annulé en 1975.**
The tunnel which the British cancelled in 1975 has already been forgotten.

The use of on is essential in the case of verbs after which the preposition 'to' is used or implied – **donner à** (to give to), **dire à** (to tell, to say to), **répondre à** (to reply to, to answer), **demander à** (to ask). Although we can say in English 'I've been given', 'he's been told', 'the letter has been answered', 'she's been asked,' and so on, this construction is impossible in French. You must use **on**:

**On m'a dit qu'il y aura un train toutes les trois minutes.**
I've been told there will be a train every three minutes.
**On lui a demandé ce qu'il pensait du projet.**
He was asked what he thought of the project.
**On a déjà répondu à la lettre.**
The letter has already been answered.

**2** By using the active instead:

**La construction d'un lien fixe trans-Manche a créé beaucoup d'emplois.**
Many jobs have been created by the building of a cross-Channel fixed link.

11

**3** Occasionally by using a reflexive verb:

**Cela ne se vend pas en France.**
That's not sold in France.

## VOCABULARY

| | |
|---|---|
| **le continent** | continent |
| **la traversée** | crossing |
| **la république** | republic |
| **la décision** | decision |
| **l'importance (f.)** | importance |
| **ferroviaire** | rail |
| **routier, routière (f.)** | road |
| **historique** | historic |
| **étranger, étrangère (f.)** | foreign |
| **relier** | to link |
| **annoncer** | to announce |
| **souligner** | to emphasise |

## IRREGULAR VERB

**construire** (to build)

Present tense
**je construis**
**tu construis**
**il/elle construit**
**nous construisons**
**vous construisez**
**ils/elles construisent**

Perfect tense
**j'ai construit**, etc

**11**

## Exercise 60

Britain and France took the decision to build the Channel Tunnel in 1986. Read the following sentences, taken from a newspaper article published at the time. Then change them into the passive:

1 Le président de la République française a souligné l'importance de la décision.
2 Un tunnel ferroviaire reliera la Grande-Bretagne au continent en 1993.
3 On construira plus tard un lien routier.
4 On a annoncé cette décision historique à Lille.
5 La traversée de la Manche a souvent découragé les touristes étrangers.

## 71 THE PRESENT PARTICIPLE

The present participle in English ends in -ing, and it is often preceded by 'while', 'on', 'by', 'in'; in French it ends in **-ant** and is often preceded by **en**:

**Il s'est cassé la jambe, en jouant au football.**
He broke his leg while playing soccer.
**En étudiant un peu tous les jours, vous apprendrez le français en trois mois.**
By studying a little every day, you will learn French in three months.

The present participle can be used, as in English, without a preceding preposition:

**Voyant que le patron était de bonne humeur, il a demandé une augmentation de salaire.**
Seeing that the boss was in a good mood, he asked for an increase in salary.

11

The present participle is formed by removing the **-ons** from the first person plural of the present tense and adding **-ant**:

| | |
|---|---|
| **chantant** | singing |
| **finissant** | finishing |
| **vendant** | selling |
| **écrivant** | writing |

There are three exceptions; **avoir**, **être**, and **savoir**:

| | |
|---|---|
| **ayant** | having |
| **étant** | being |
| **sachant** | knowing |

Remember that **en** is the only preposition that is followed by the present participle in French; all others are followed by the infinitive (see week 10, section 62).

Remember also that sentences such as 'I am going', 'I am watching', 'I am listening' are translated by the present tense (see week 2, section 8):

| | |
|---|---|
| **je vais** | I'm going |
| **je regarde** | I'm watching |
| **j'écoute** | I'm listening |

11

## VOCABULARY

| | |
|---|---|
| **le bras** | arm |
| **le cours** | course, class |
| **le diplôme** | diploma |
| **l'agent de police** | policeman |
| **la fois** | time, occasion |
| **la réponse** | reply |
| **blessé** | injured |
| **par** | per |
| **faire du ski** | to ski |
| | |
| **tomber** | to fall (conjugated with **être**) |
| **patiner** | to skate |
| **appeler** | to call (see section 81) |

## IRREGULAR VERB

**voir** (to see)

Present tense
**je vois**
**tu vois**
**il/elle voit**
**nous voyons**
**vous voyez**
**ils/elles voient**

Perfect tense
**j'ai vu**, etc

Future tense
**je verrai**, etc

## Exercise 61

Combine the following using a present participle:

1 Elle s'est cassé le bras. Elle faisait du ski.
2 Je suis tombé. Je patinais.
3 Il allait aux cours du soir trois fois par semaine.
  Il a obtenu son diplôme.
4 L'agent de police a vu que l'automobiliste était
  blessé. Il a appelé une ambulance.
5 Vous téléphonez. Vous aurez la réponse tout de suite.

11

WEEK 11 | **179**

## 72 MORE ABOUT THE IMPERATIVE

The imperative of **avoir** and **être** is:

| | | | |
|---|---|---|---|
| **aie** | have (fam.) | **sois** | be (fam.) |
| **ayez** | have | **soyez** | be |
| **ayons** | let's have | **soyons** | let's be |

Examples:
**Ayez un peu de patience.** Have a little patience.
**Ne soyez pas en retard.** Don't be late.
**Soyons raisonnables.** Let's be reasonable.

## 73 THE IMPERATIVE WITH PRONOUNS

Look at the following sentences:

**Invitez votre secrétaire au restaurant.**
Invite your secretary to the restaurant.
**Invitez-la.**
Invite her.
**Ne l'invitez pas.**
Don't invite her.

**Donnez le numéro de téléphone aux clients.**
Give the telephone number to the clients.
**Donnez-leur le numéro.**
Give them the number.
**Ne leur donnez pas le numéro.**
Don't give them the number.

**Asseyez-vous dans ce fauteuil.**
Sit down in this armchair.
**Ne vous asseyez pas dans ce fauteuil.**
Don't sit down in this armchair.

You will have noticed that pronouns follow the verb in the affirmative imperative, while pronouns precede the verb in the negative imperative.

11

Now study the following:

**Donnez-moi votre adresse.**
**Donnez-la-moi.**
**Ne me donnez pas votre adresse.**
**Ne me la donnez pas.**
**Couche-toi.**
**Ne te couche pas.**

You will have noticed that **me** and **te** become **moi** and **toi** in the affirmative imperative, and that in the affirmative imperative we say **donnez-le-moi, envoyez-la-moi, montrez-les-moi**.

Of course, telling people to do things can be made more polite by being phrased as a question, using one of the following expressions in front of the infinitive:

| | |
|---|---|
| **Voulez-vous ...?** | Will you ...? |
| **Voulez-vous bien ...?** | Would you kindly ...? |
| **Pourriez-vous ...?** | Could you ...? |

Examples:
**Voulez-vous signer ici, s'il vous plaît?**
Will you sign here please?
**Voulez-vous bien passer à la caisse, s'il vous plaît?**
Would you kindly go to the cashdesk please?
**Pourriez-vous nous apporter encore du café?**
Could you bring us some more coffee?

11

## Exercise 62

Imagine you're asking your secretary to carry out a number of tasks. The trouble is you keep changing your mind!

Translate:

1 Telephone him – no, don't telephone him.
2 Send them this brochure – no, don't send it to them.
3 Copy this document – no, don't copy it.
4 Give me the catalogue– no, don't give it to me.
5 Send her the samples – no, don't send them to her.
6 Be here at 9 o'clock – no, at 8 o'clock.
7 Would you be so kind as to work overtime?

## 74 THE PLUPERFECT ('HE HAD GONE')

'I had telephoned', 'I had spoken', etc is expressed by using the imperfect of **avoir** or **être** with the past participle:

**J'avais déjà téléphoné à l'hôpital.**
I had already telephoned the hospital.
**Elle était déjà partie, quand son mari est arrivé.**
She had already left, when her husband arrived.

**11**

## 75 'DEPUIS' ('SINCE')

The French sometimes use the present tense where we use the past tense in English. This happens when an action, which began in the past, is still continuing in the present:

**Depuis quand êtes-vous en France?**
How long have you been in France? (lit. 'Since when are you in France?')
**Depuis combien de temps apprenez-vous le français?**
How long have you been learning French?
**Je suis en France depuis une semaine, mais j'apprends le français depuis trois mois.**
I've been in France for a week, but I've been learning French for three months.

## 76 'VENIR DE' ('TO HAVE JUST ...')

This idiomatic expression, used only in the present and imperfect tenses, expresses the idea of 'having just done something':

**Je viens d'acheter une maison.**
I have just bought a house.
**Elle venait de vendre son appartement.**
She had just sold her flat.

11

## Exercice 63

Translate:

1 I've been married for five years.
2 I've lived in this house for four years.
3 I've worked for this bank for three years.
4 I've had this car for two years.
5 I've been learning to play the piano for one year.

## Exercice 64

Answer the questions as follows:

Allez-vous téléphoner à la police?
    Are you going to telephone the police?

Mais je viens de téléphoner à la police.
    But I've just telephoned the police.

1 Allez-vous appeler un docteur?
2 Allez-vous prévenir les pompiers?
3 Pouvez-vous me montrer votre permis de conduire?
4 Est-ce que les ambulanciers vont transporter les blessés à l'hôpital?
5 Est-ce que vous allez me donner votre adresse?

11

## VOCABULARY

| | |
|---|---|
| **le volant** | steering wheel |
| **l'isolement (m.)** | isolation |
| **la fin** | end |
| **l'île (f.)** | island |
| **la façon** | way |
| **de toutes façons** | anyay |
| **faciliter** | make easy |
| **construire** | to build |
| **l'entente (f.)** | understanding |
| **nécessaire** | necessary |
| **contre** | against |
| **cordial** | cordial |
| **jurer** | to swear |
| **vive ...!** | long live ...! |

## IRREGULAR VERB

**vivre** (to live)

Present tense
**je vis**
**tu vis**
**il/elle vit**
**nous vivons**
**vous vivez**
**ils/elles vivent**

Perfect tense
**j'ai vécu**, etc

## CONVERSATION

*Le tunnel sous la Manche*

Une conversation entre un Anglais et une Française

FRANÇAISE  **On dit que le tunnel sous la Manche est un vrai succès pour nos deux pays. Qu'en pensez-vous?**

ANGLAIS  **Oui, c'est vrai. Mais pourqui construire un tunnel ferroviaire? Quand Mme Thatcher était premier ministre britannique, elle avait juré qu'elle serait la première à traverser la Manche au volant de sa voiture.**

FRANÇAISE  **C'est possible, mais elle n'est plus premier ministre depuis longtemps. De toutes façons, les voitures utilisent le train pour traverser la Manche, avec le Shuttle. Ça marche bien, je trouve. Qu'est-ce que vous pensez vous-même du tunnel?**

ANGLAIS  **Eh bien, en construisant ce tunnel, on a mis fin à l'isolement de la Grande-Bretagne, et en même temps on a créé de nouveaux emplois. Mais on a aussi facilité l'immigration clandestine.**

FRANÇAISE  **Y a-t-il donc des gens qui sont contre le tunnel?**

ANGLAIS  **Oui, il y a des gens qui pensent que la Grande-Bretagne aurait dû rester une île. Je ne suis pas sûr qu'ils aient raison.**

FRANÇAISE  **De toutes façons, avec un tunnel ou sans tunnel – vive l'Entente cordiale!**

11

*The Tunnel under the Channel*

A conversation between an Englishman and a Frenchwoman

FRENCHWOMAN  It is said that the Channel has been a real success for both our countries. What do you think?

ENGLISHMAN  Yes, it's true. But why a rail tunnel? When Mrs Thatcher was British Prime Minister, she swore that she would be the first to cross the Channel at the wheel of her car.

FRENCHWOMAN  Yes, but she hasn't been Prime Minister for a long time. In any case cars use the train to cross the Channel with the Shuttle. It works well, I find. What do you yourself think of the tunnel?

ENGLISHMAN  Well, by building the tunnel we have put an end to Britain's isolation, and at the same time we have created new jobs. But we have also made illegal immigration easier.

FRENCHWOMAN  Are there people who are against the Tunnel?

ENGLISHMAN  Yes, there are people who think that Great Britain should have remained an island. I am not sure they're right.

FRENCHWOMAN  Anyway, with a tunnel or without a tunnel – long live the Entente Cordiale!

11

# Week 12

- *the use of 'faire' in its variety of meanings*
- *the past historic tense in both regular and irregular verbs*
- *verbs needing/not needing a preposition*
- *spelling changes in verbs (to keep them regular)*
- *the subjunctive mood, used to express a wish or suggestion*

## 77 THE MANY USES OF THE VERB 'FAIRE'

**Faire** is the most overworked verb in the French language. It is conjugated as follows:

Present tense
**je fais**
**tu fais**
**il/elle fait**
**nous faisons**
**vous faites**
**ils/elles font**

Perfect tense
**j'ai fait**

Imperfect tense
**je faisais**

Future tense
**je ferai**

**Faire** can have a variety of meanings, as shown in the following examples:

to do:
**Qu'est-ce que vous faites dans la vie?**
What do you do for a living?

to make:
**Ma mère va faire un gâteau.**
My mother is going to make a cake.

to give:
**Je vais faire une conférence sur la graphologie.**
I'm going to give a lecture on graphology.

to take:
**Elle aime faire une promenade au parc.**
She likes to take a walk in the park.

to have:
**Mon mari fait de la tension.**
My husband has high blood pressure.

to act:
**Ne fais pas l'idiot.**
Don't act the fool.

to force:
**Je l'ai fait travailler.**
I forced him to work (or I made him work).

to have something done:
**Ils font construire une maison.**
They're having a house built.

**Faire** is also used to talk about the weather (see section 42):
**Il fait beau.**
The weather is fine.

It is used in many idiomatic expressions:
**Tu me fais marcher.**
You're pulling my leg.

## Exercise 65

Rewrite the following using the verb faire:

1 Quelle est votre profession?
2 Ma soeur prépare une tarte aux pommes.
3 Je vais parler de la psychologie devant 200 personnes.
4 Elle s'est promenée au parc hier.
5 Il a de la fièvre.
6 Ne sois pas bête.
7 J'ai forcé mon fils à travailler.
8 On me construit une maison à Avignon.

## 78 THE PAST HISTORIC

There is a past tense that you will meet when reading books, magazines and newspapers, but almost never in conversation, which is called the past historic or past definite. It is a literary tense and you yourself will never need to use it, but you must be able to recognise it. The past historic describes a completed action in the past and, in the case of regular verbs, is formed by removing the **-er**, **-ir**, **-re** from the infinitive and adding the following endings:

12

| -er verbs | | -ir/-re verbs | |
|---|---|---|---|
| je | -ai | je | -is |
| tu | -as | tu | -is |
| il/elle | -a | il/elle | -it |
| nous | -âmes | nous | -îmes |
| vous | -âtes | vous | -îtes |
| ils/elles | -èrent | ils/elles | -irent |

Examples:

**Le lendemain Paul arriva tôt.**
The following day Paul arrived early.
**Les touristes visitèrent cinq pays en cinq jours.**
The tourists visited five countries in five days.
**Victor Hugo finit d'écrire *Les Misérables* en 1862.**
Victor Hugo finished writing *Les Misérables* in 1862.

## 79 THE PAST HISTORIC OF IRREGULAR VERBS

You will sometimes be able to recognise the past historic of irregular verbs by the similarity to the past participle:

| Infinitive | Perfect tense | Past historic | Meaning |
|---|---|---|---|
| **dire** | **j'ai dit** | **je dis** | I said |
| **mettre** | **j'ai mis** | **je mis** | I put |
| **prendre** | **j'ai pris** | **je pris** | I took |
| **sortir** | **je suis sorti** | **je sortis** | I went out |
| **avoir** | **j'ai eu** | **j'eus** | I had |
| **lire** | **j'ai lu** | **je lus** | I read |
| **vivre** | **j'ai vécu** | **je vécus** | I lived |

Other irregular forms just have to be learned:

| Infinitive | Perfect tense | Past historic | Meaning |
|---|---|---|---|
| **écrire** | **j'ai écrit** | **j'écrivis** | I wrote |
| **être** | **j'ai été** | **je fus** | I was |
| **faire** | **j'ai fait** | **je fis** | I did |
| **venir** | **je suis venu** | **je vins** | I came |
| **voir** | **j'ai vu** | **je vis** | I saw |

12

## Exercise 66

Translate into English:

| | | | |
|---|---|---|---|
| **1** | Il donna. | **6** | Vous eûtes. |
| **2** | Je vendis. | **7** | Il prit. |
| **3** | Nous finîmes. | **8** | Elle sortit. |
| **4** | Elle eut. | **9** | Ils lurent. |
| **5** | Je fus. | **10** | Elles mirent. |

## 80 VERBS WITH OR WITHOUT A PREPOSITION

Although a preposition is necessary in English to complete the meaning of the following English verbs, none is required in French:

| | |
|---|---|
| to approve of | **approuver** |
| to listen to | **écouter** |
| to look at | **regarder** |
| to look for | **chercher** |
| to ask for | **demander** |
| to pay for | **payer** |
| to wait for | **attendre** |

Conversely, a preposition is sometimes needed in French but not in English:

| | |
|---|---|
| **demander à** | to ask |
| **dire à** | to tell |
| **défendre à** | to forbid |
| **obéir à** | to obey |
| **permettre à** | to allow |
| **ressembler à** | to resemble |
| **toucher à** | to touch |
| **jouer à** | to play (game) |
| **jouer de** | to play (instrument) |

Examples:
**J'ai écouté les explications du guide avec attention.**
I listened carefully to the guide's explanations.

12

**Regardez la cathédrale à droite.**
Look at the cathedral on the right.
**Attendez les autres membres du groupe.**
Wait for the other members of the group.
**Nous cherchons les toilettes.**
We are looking for the toilets.
**Je vais demander deux billets d'entrée.**
I'm going to ask for two admission tickets.
**Il aime jouer au tennis.**
He likes to play tennis.
**Elle aime jouer du piano.**
She likes to play the piano.

## 81 SPELLING CHANGES

In French, we sometimes have to make changes in the spelling of different forms of the same verb, so that the basic sound of the verb will remain unchanged. Let's take an example:

We have learned that we form the present tense by removing the -er from the infinitive and adding certain endings, and in the case of nous we add -ons. But if we do this with the verb **manger** (to eat), pronounced 'mah*ng*-zhay', we will have '**mangons**', pronounced 'mah*ng*-gong' i.e. a change in the basic sound. So, in order to keep the soft sound 'zh' we must add an **e** and we write **nous mangeons**. This spelling change takes place whenever the **g** is followed by **o** or **a**:

| | | |
|---|---|---|
| **nous mangeons** | we eat | (present tense) |
| **je mangeais** | I was eating | (imperfect) |
| **il mangea** | he ate | (past historic) |
| **en mangeant** | while eating | (present participle) |

Here are some important verbs that behave like manger:

| | |
|---|---|
| **arranger** | to arrange |
| **corriger** | to correct |
| **décourager** | to discourage |

**12**

| | |
|---|---|
| **encourager** | to encourage |
| **déranger** | to disturb |
| **nager** | to swim |
| **voyager** | to travel |

Everything that has been said about keeping the **g** soft also applies to the soft **c** in a verb like **annoncer** (to announce). In order to keep the **c** soft in the **nous**-form, we have to add a cedilla to the **c** and we write **nous annonçons**. If we don't do this, the pronunciation will be 'ah-no*ng*-ko*ng*'. So, we write **ç** before **o** and **a**:

| | |
|---|---|
| **nous annonçons** | we announce |
| **j'annonçais** | I was announcing |
| **il annonça** | he announced |
| **en annonçant** | while announcing |

Important verbs like **annoncer**:

| | |
|---|---|
| **commencer** | to begin |
| **divorcer** | to divorce |
| **prononcer** | to pronounce |
| **remplacer** | to replace |

Some verbs whose infinitive ends in **-eler** and **-eter** double the **l** and **t** before a silent **e**:

**appeler** (to call)

Present tense
| | |
|---|---|
| **j'appelle** | **nous appelons** |
| **tu appelles** | **vous appelez** |
| **il/elle appelle** | **ils/elles appellent** |

Future tense
**j'appellerai**

Conditional tense
**j'appellerais**

**12**

Important verbs like **appeler**:

| | |
|---|---|
| **rappeler** | to call back, to remind |
| **renouveler** | to renew |
| **jeter** | to throw |

Some verbs change **e** to **è** before a silent **e**:

**acheter** (to buy)

Present tense

| | |
|---|---|
| **j'achète** | **nous achetons** |
| **tu achètes** | **vous achetez** |
| **il/elle achète** | **ils/elles achètent** |

Future tense
**j'achèterai**

Conditional tense
**j'achèterais**

Important verbs like **acheter**:

| | |
|---|---|
| **lever** | to raise |
| **se lever** | to get up |
| **mener** | to lead |
| **amener** | to bring |

Some verbs change **é** to **è** before a silent **e** (present tense and present subjunctive only):

**espérer** (to hope)

Present tense

| | |
|---|---|
| **j'espère** | **nous espérons** |
| **tu espères** | **vous espérez** |
| **il/elle espère** | **ils/elles espèrent** |

Important verbs like **espérer**:

| | |
|---|---|
| **considérer** | to consider |

12

| **régler** | to settle |
| **répéter** | to repeat |
| **s'inquiéter** | to worry |
| **préférer** | to prefer |

Verbs whose infinitive ends in **-yer** change **y** to **i** before a silent **e**:

**nettoyer** (to clean)

Present tense

| **je nettoie** | **nous nettoyons** |
| **tu nettoies** | **vous nettoyez** |
| **il/elle nettoie** | **ils/elles nettoient** |

Future tense
**je nettoierai**

Conditional tense
**je nettoierais**

Important verbs like **nettoyer**:

| **employer** | to use |
| **s'ennuyer** | to be bored |
| **envoyer** | to send  (Future: **j'enverrai**) |
| **payer** | to pay (optional spelling change) |
| **essayer** | to try (optional spelling change) |

## 82 THE SUBJUNCTIVE

We have a subjunctive mood in English, although it is used much less often than in French. In English, when we make a suggestion or express a wish, we use the subjunctive. For example, when we say 'I suggest that a vote be taken' or 'I wish today were Saturday', 'be' and 'were' are subjunctives.

In French, we use the subjunctive after verbs and expressions which denote:

**12**

| a wish | **vouloir, désirer** | to want, to wish |
|---|---|---|
| a preference | **préférer** | to prefer |
| a suggestion | **suggérer, proposer** | to suggest |
| a necessity | **falloir** | to be necessary |
| a demand | **exiger** | to demand |
| surprise | **être surpris** | to be surprised |
| regret | **regretter** | to regret |
| anger | **être furieux** | to be furious |
| fear | **avoir peur** | to be afraid |
| doubt | **douter** | to doubt |
| possibility | **être possible** | to be possible |
| pleasure | **être content** | to be pleased |
| sorrow | **être désolé** | to be sorry |

The subjunctive is always preceded by **que** (that). It is formed by removing the **-ent** ending from the third person plural form of the present tense and adding:

| **je** | **-e** | **nous** | **-ions** |
|---|---|---|---|
| **tu** | **-es** | **vous** | **-iez** |
| **il/elle** | **-e** | **ils/elles** | **-ent** |

Examples:

| **… que je parle** | **… que nous vendions** |
|---|---|
| **… que tu donnes** | **… que vous répondiez** |
| **… qu'il finisse** | **… qu'ils mettent** |
| **… qu'elle maigrisse** | **… qu'elles permettent** |

Examples of the use of the subjunctive:
**Je voudrais que vous me fixiez un rendez-vous chez le coiffeur.**
I would like you to fix an appointment for me at the hairdresser's.
**Je voudrais que vous me coupiez les cheveux.**
I would like you to cut my hair.
**Je préfère qu'il ne me coupe pas les cheveux trop court.**
I prefer him not to cut my hair too short.
**Je veux qu'il me rase.**
I want him to shave me.

12

**Il faut que vous me mettiez un peu de laque (f.) sur les cheveux à cause du vent.**
You must put a little hair spray on my hair because of the wind.
**Je suis surpris(e) que le coiffeur ne vende pas de peignes (m.).**
I am surprised that the hairdresser doesn't sell combs.
**Je suis content(e) que vous me parliez en français.**
I am pleased that you are talking to me in French.

It is important to note that when the subject of the dependent verb is the same as that of the main verb, the construction with an infinitive is used. Compare:

**Je voudrais partir.**  I'd like to leave.
**Nous voudrions partir.**  We'd like to leave.
*But*
**Nous voudrions que vous partiez.** We'd like you to leave.

There are some irregular subjunctives, and the most important are:

| | |
|---|---|
| **être** (to be) | **que je sois, il soit, nous soyons, ils soient** |
| **avoir** (to have) | **que j'aie, il ait, nous ayons, ils aient** |
| **aller** (to go) | **que j'aille, il aille, nous allions, ils aillent** |
| **faire** (to do, make) | **que je fasse, il fasse, nous fassions, ils fassent** |
| **pouvoir** (to be able) | **que je puisse, il puisse, nous puissions, ils puissent** |
| **prendre** (to take) | **que je prenne, il prenne, nous prenions, ils prennent** |
| **savoir** (to know) | **que je sache, il sache, nous sachions, ils sachent** |
| **venir** (to come) | **que je vienne, il vienne, nous venions, ils viennent** |

12

The subjunctive is also used after the following conjunctions – those marked * require **ne** before the verb:

| | |
|---|---|
| **quoique** | although |
| **bien que** | although |
| **pour que** | in order that |
| **afin que** | in order that |
| **de peur que*** | for fear that |
| **à condition que** | on condition that |
| **pourvu que** | provided that |
| **jusqu'à ce que** | until |
| **à moins que*** | unless |
| **avant que*** | before |

Examples:

**Bien qu'il sache parler français, il refuse de téléphoner à Paris.**

Although he can speak French, he refuses to telephone Paris.

**Je vous ai acheté ce portable pour que vous puissiez me parler de temps en temps.**

I've bought you this mobile phone so that you can speak to me from time to time.

**Je veux bien vous donner les CD, à condition que vous étudiez chaque soir.**

I'm quite willing to give you the CDs, on condition that you study every evening.

**A moins que vous ne m'aidiez, je ne pourrai pas finir cet exercice.**

Unless you help me, I won't be able to finish this exercise.

**Je dois rester ici jusqu'à ce que ma femme arrive.**

I must stay here until my wife arrives.

The subjunctive is also used after:

**1** a superlative:

**C'est la plus grande librairie que nous ayons jamais vue.**

This is the biggest bookshop we have ever seen.

**2 seul** (only), **premier** (first), **dernier** (last):

**Paul est le seul qui puisse aller à la réunion.**

Paul is the only one who can go to the meeting.

12

**3** an indefinite antecedent:
**Je cherche un médecin qui sache parler anglais.**
I'm looking for a doctor who can speak English.
(i.e. I'm not sure that one exists)
*But*
**Je cherche le médecin qui sait parler anglais.**
I'm looking for the doctor who can speak English.
(i.e. I know he exists)

**4** impersonal verbs such as:

| | |
|---|---|
| **Il faut que …** | It is necessary that … |
| **Il vaut mieux que …** | It is better that … |
| **Il est important que …** | It is important that … |
| **Il est possible que …** | It is possible that … |
| **Il est inévitable que …** | It is inevitable that … |
| **Il est dommage que …** | It is a pity that … |

Examples:
**Il est important que nous réservions les chambres à l'avance.**
It is important that we reserve the rooms in advance.
**Il est dommage qu'il ne vienne pas aujourd'hui.**
It is a pity that he's not coming today.

**5** the negative of **penser** (to think) and **croire** (to believe) – compare:
**Je pense que Caroline va à la réception.**
I think that Caroline is going to the reception.
**Je ne pense pas que Caroline aille à la réception.**
I don't think Caroline is going to the reception.

**6 quoi que** (whatever):
**… quoi que vous fassiez …**
… whatever you do …

**7 quel que, quelle que, quels que, quelles que**
(whatever):
**… quelle que soit la raison …**
… whatever the reason may be …

12

The subjunctive is also used for the third person imperative:

**Qu'il prenne le parapluie.**  Let him take the umbrella.
**Qu'elle parte.**  Let her leave.
**Qu'ils fassent la vaisselle.**  Let them do the washing-up.

Note that there is also a perfect subjunctive which is used for action in the past. The perfect subjunctive is formed with **avoir** or **être**:

**Je suis content que vous ayez retrouvé votre portefeuille.**
I am pleased that you have found your wallet.
**Je suis désolé qu'elle soit tombée malade.**
I am sorry that she has fallen ill.

## VOCABULARY

| | |
|---|---|
| **le lancement** | launching |
| **le vaisseau spatial** | spacecraft |
| **le discours** | speech |
| **l'espace (m.)** | space |
| **la déclaration** | statement |
| **la conquête** | conquest |
| **la mission** | mission |
| **l'apesanteur (f.)** | weightlessness |
| **l'expérience (f.)** | experiment, experience |
| **les données (f.)** | data |
| **continuer** | to continue |
| **participer** | to take part |
| **filmer** | to film |
| **enregistrer** | to record |
| **reporter** | to postpone |
| **mener** | to conduct |
| **avoir lieu** | to take place |
| **en direct** | live |
| **quand même** | still, nevertheless |

12

## Exercise 67

Translate:

1  I suggest that the President make a statement on television.

2  We must continue our conquest of space.

3  He would like the launching of the spacecraft to take place next week.

4  I am pleased that you are taking part in this space mission.

5  It is important that the launching should be filmed live.

6  Unless you can give me all the data recorded by the computers, I cannot take a decision.

7  We are pleased that the President has decided to postpone his speech.

8  Although the astronauts are used to weightlessness, they still have a little difficulty carrying out their experiments on board the spacecraft.

12

## VOCABULARY

| | |
|---|---|
| **le/la graphologue** | graphologist |
| **le mariage** | wedding, marriage |
| **le(s) renseignement(s) (m.)** | information |
| **l'échantillon (m.)** | sample |
| **la conversation téléphonique** | telephone conversation |
| **la personnalité** | personality |
| **la conclusion** | conclusion |
| **l'écriture (f.)** | handwriting |
| **l'analyse (f.)** | analysis |
| **les félicitations (f.)** | congratulations |
| **analyser** | analyse |
| **rédiger** | to write, compose |
| **retarder** | to delay |
| **tout à fait** | quite, completely |
| **compatible** | compatible |
| **ordinaire** | ordinary |
| **favorable** | favourable |
| **alors** | so |
| **allô** | hello (on the telephone) |

12

Une conversation téléphonique entre un graphologue et une jeune cliente.

CLIENTE  **Allô. Bonjour, Monsieur. C'est vous le graphologue?**

GRAPHOLOGUE  **Oui, c'est moi.**

CLIENTE  **Eh bien, mon fiancé vient de fixer la date de notre mariage et ...**

GRAPHOLOGUE  **Félicitations, Mademoiselle!**

CLIENTE  **Merci. Je ne crois pas que je sois tout à fait prête pour le mariage, alors je voudrais que vous analysiez mon écriture et aussi celle de mon fiancé pour voir si nos personnalités sont compatibles.**

GRAPHOLOGUE  **Oui, c'est très facile. Il faut que vous m'envoyiez un échantillon de votre écriture et de celle de votre fiancé.**

CLIENTE  **Quelle sorte d'échantillon faut-il que je vous envoie?**

GRAPHOLOGUE  **Je préfère que vous écriviez une lettre tout à fait ordinaire, mais il faut qu'elle soit signée.**

CLIENTE  **Je doute que mon fiancé soit prêt à rédiger une lettre et à la signer sans savoir pourquoi.**

GRAPHOLOGUE  **Mais il est très important qu'il n'en connaisse pas la raison.**

CLIENTE  **Bon, très bien. Pour que vous puissiez arriver à une conclusion plus rapidement, est-ce qu'il faut que nous vous donnions des renseignements supplémentaires?**

GRAPHOLOGUE  **Non, pas du tout.**

CLIENTE  **Vous savez, cette analyse est très importante pour moi. A moins que votre rapport ne soit favorable, il est possible que je retarde le mariage.**

**12**

A telephone conversation between a graphologist and a young client.

CLIENT  Hallo. Good morning. Are you the graphologist?

GRAPHOLOGIST  Yes, I am.

CLIENT  Well, my fiancé has just fixed the date of our wedding and …

GRAPHOLOGIST  Congratulations!

CLIENT  Thank you. I don't think I'm quite ready for marriage, so I'd like you to analyse my handwriting, and also my fiancé's, in order to see if our personalities are compatible.

GRAPHOLOGIST  Yes, that's very easy. You must send me a sample of your handwriting and your fiancé's.

CLIENT  What sort of sample do I have to send?

GRAPHOLOGIST  I prefer you to write a perfectly ordinary letter, but it must be signed.

CLIENT  I doubt whether my fiancé will be willing to write a letter and to sign it without knowing why.

GRAPHOLOGIST  But it's very important that he doesn't know the reason for it.

CLIENT  OK, fine. So that you can come to a conclusion more rapidly, do we have to give you any additional information?

GRAPHOLOGIST  No, not at all.

CLIENT  You know, this analysis is very important for me. Unless your report is favourable, it's possible I may delay the wedding.

12

The following four exercises are not an essential part of the 'Three Months' course, but you will certainly consolidate your knowledge of French if you make the effort to complete them. Do the Self-assessment test 3 first.

## Exercise 68

Translate back into French all the English translations of the CONVERSATIONS which have appeared in this book.

## Exercise 69

Translate back into French all the English translations of the EXAMPLES which have appeared in this book.

## Exercise 70

Translate back into French all the English translations of the VOCABULARY LISTS which have appeared in this book.

## Exercise 71

Translate back into English all the sentences in the KEY TO EXERCISES.

12

# Self-assessment test 3 A–C

This self-assessment test, based on weeks 9–12, will enable you to check on your progress and to see whether any revision is needed. Deduct one mark for every grammatical mistake or wrong spelling. The answers and score assessment are in the Key.

**A** Reflexive verbs    Total: 11 marks

Give the French for these sentences describing daily routines and what happened yesterday:

1  I wake up at 8 a.m.
2  I wash.
3  I shave.
4  I go to work.
5  Monique gets up at 9 o'clock.
6  She washes.
7  She dresses quickly.
8  She goes to the office.
9  Nicole and I (f.) woke up at 10 o'clock.
10  We put on our make-up.
11  We went to the station.

**B** Verbs preceded by prepositions    Total: 4 marks

Complete the following:

1  Il est parti [without saying] un mot.
2  Elle a hésité [before replying].
3  J'ai commencé [by criticising] l'interprète.
4  [After having bought] un ordinateur, il a travaillé plus vite.

**C** Conjunctions    Total: 5 marks

Complete the following sentences with the most suitable conjunction:

1  Nous avons acheté une tente, … nous voulons faire du camping.
2  Mon père n'aime pas l'Italie, … nous sommes allés en Allemagne.
3  … tu vas chercher de la bière, je vais regarder la télévision.
4  C'est un bon camping, … où sont les toilettes?
5  … vous serez prêts, je préparerai à manger.

12

## Self-assessment test 3  D–G

**D** Numbers    Total: 12 marks
Complete the following, writing the totals in words:

**A**  320 + 120          **D**  260 + 50
**B**  150 + 150          **E**  1000 + 330
**C**  580 + 200          **F**  450 + 50

**E** Peculiarities of French construction    Total: 10 marks
Give the French for:

**1** How long have you been in England? (Use 'tu')
**2** I've been working here since the 2nd May.
**3** We've been learning French for three months.
**4** We've just bought an apartment.
**5** They've just called a doctor.

**F** Translation of 'to' before an infinitive    Total: 6 marks
Complete the following:

**1** [We hope to] aller à la plage.
**2** [They've decided to] louer une voiture.
**3** [They (f.) are pleased to] voir le soleil.
**4** [She intends to] acheter des lunettes de soleil.
**5** [I hesitate to] faire du ski nautique.
**6** [Will you (tu) have the opportunity to] faire de la planche à voile?

**G** The verb 'faire'    Total: 4 marks
Rewrite the following, using faire:

**1** Quelle est votre profession?
**2** Ma mère prépare un gâteau.
**3** Je vais parler de la conquête de l'espace devant 100 personnes.
**4** Il s'est promené au parc.

**12**

# Self-assessment test 3  H–J

**H** The imperative (with pronouns)    Total: 16 marks
Make up your mind! Give the French for:

1 (the letter) Copy it – no, don't copy it.
2 (the samples) Send them – no, don't send them.
3 (the catalogue) Give it to me – no, don't give it to me.
4 Telephone them – no, don't telephone them.

**I** The subjunctive    Total: 8 marks
Complete the following:

1 Je voudrais que [you fix] un rendez-vous.
2 Je veux bien vous aider, à condition que [you finish] le travail aujourd'hui.
3 Il est dommage que [Sophie isn't coming] à la réception.
4 Nous sommes contents que [they've found] une petite  maison.

**J** Conversation (Role-play)    Total: 24 marks
Take the part of Nicole:

PAUL   Est-ce que tu écoutes toujours les CD que tu as achetés récemment?

NICOLE   Yes, of course. I bought them because I have to learn English in three months.

PAUL   Est-ce que tu as le temps d'écouter ces CD?

NICOLE   Yes. If I listen to them in the morning when I'm washing. My husband listens to them as well, when he's shaving. If I succeed in learning English, it'll be possible for me to get promotion and travel to the United States.

12

# Reading practice

These extracts from French literature and modern journals each
have an English translation on the facing page. Refer to this as
little as possible during your first reading of the French, then go
through the piece again, noting constructions and vocabulary.

## Les Misérables

L'hôpital était une maison étroite et basse à un seul étage
avec un petit jardin.

Trois jours après son arrivée, l'évêque visita l'hôpital.
La visite terminée, il fit prier le directeur de vouloir bien venir
jusque chez lui.

– Monsieur le directeur de l'hôpital, lui dit-il, combien en
ce moment avez-vous de malades?

– Vingt-six, monseigneur.

– C'est ce que j'avais compté, dit l'évêque.

– Les lits, reprit le directeur, sont bien serrés les uns contre
les autres.

– C'est ce que j'avais remarqué.

– Les salles ne sont que des chambres et l'air s'y renouvelle
difficilement.

– C'est ce qui me semble.

– Et puis, quand il y a un rayon de soleil, le jardin est bien petit
pour les convalescents.

– C'est bien ce que je me disais.

– Dans les épidémies, nous avons eu cette année le typhus, nous
avons eu la suette militaire il y a deux ans; cent malades
quelquefois, nous ne savons que faire.

– C'est la pensée qui m'était venue.

– Que voulez-vous, monseigneur? dit le directeur, il faut se
résigner.

Cette conversation avait lieu dans la salle à manger-galerie du
rez-de-chaussée.

L'évêque garda un moment de silence, puis il se tourna
brusquement vers le directeur de l'hôpital.

– Monsieur, dit-il, combien pensez-vous qu'il tiendrait de lits
rien que dans cette salle?

– Dans la salle à manger de monseigneur? s'écria le directeur
stupéfait.

L'évêque parcourait la salle du regard et semblait y faire avec les
yeux des mesures et des calculs.

– Il y tiendrait bien vingt lits ! dit-il, comme se parlant à lui-
même, puis élevant la voix:

# Les Misérables

The hospital was a narrow and low two-storeyed house with a small garden.

Three days after his arrival, the bishop visited the hospital. When the visit was over, he asked the director to be good enough to come home with him.

'Director,' he said to him, 'how many patients do you have at this moment?'

'Twenty six, Monseigneur.'

'That's how many I counted,' said the bishop.

'The beds,' continued the director, 'are very close to each other.'

'I noticed.'

'The wards are only bedrooms and the air is not very fresh.'

'I can imagine.'

'And when we do get some sunshine, the garden is very small for the convalescents.'

'That's what I was thinking.'

'When we have an epidemic, this year we've had typhus and two years ago we had military fever, with up to a hundred patients sometimes, we don't know what to do.'

'That thought had occurred to me.'

'What can one do, Monseigneur?' said the director. 'We must resign ourselves to it.'

This conversation took place in the ground floor banquet-hall.

The bishop remained silent for a moment, then he suddenly turned towards the director of the hospital.

'Tell me,' he said, 'how many beds do you think this room would hold?'

'The Monseigneur's dining room?' the director cried out, astonished.

The bishop looked around the room and seemed to be taking measurements and making calculations with his eyes.

'It would certainly hold twenty beds,' he said, as if talking to himself. Then he raised his voice:

– Tenez, monsieur le directeur de l'hôpital, je vais vous dire. Il y a évidemment une erreur. Vous êtes vingt-six personnes dans cinq ou six petites chambres. Nous sommes trois ici et nous avons place pour soixante, il y a erreur, je vous dis, vous avez mon logis et j'ai le vôtre. Rendez-moi ma maison; c'est ici chez vous.

Le lendemain les vingt-six pauvres malades étaient installés dans le palais de l'évêque et l'évêque était à l'hôpital.

Taken from *Book 1, Chapter 2*
Victor Hugo (1802–1885)

'Listen, Director, I'm going to tell you something. There's obviously an error. You have twenty six people in five or six small bedrooms. There are three of us here and we have room for sixty. There's an error, I tell you. You have my house and I have yours. Give me back my house. You should be here.'

The following day the twenty six poor patients were installed in the bishop's palace and the bishop was installed in the hospital.

# Papa, l'ordinateur et moi

On connaît enfin le profil de l'Homo informaticus moyen. C'est un petit garçon qui s'est fait offrir pour Noël un micro-ordinateur à bas prix et qui y pianote cinquante minutes par jour, six jours par mois, pour lutter contre des météorites en folie. Telles sont en substance les conclusions auxquelles ont abouti les enquêteurs de la Fnac* en sondant leurs clients.

Les chiffres révélés la semaine dernière parlent d'eux-mêmes. Scénario modèle: papa (90% des acheteurs sont des hommes), influencé par ses copains, se décide à offrir un micro-ordinateur à son rejeton. Papa est en général un cadre au niveau d'instruction universitaire. Il hésite peu, ne l'essaie pas et prend en général le moins cher (le prix est pour 67% des gens le premier critère de choix, avant même le nombre de logiciels disponibles et la facilité d'utilisation). Dès qu'il arrive à la maison, papa lit la notice et annonce à tout le monde qu'il a bien l'intention de s'attaquer au basic (47% des acheteurs veulent apprendre à programmer avant l'achat). Mais cette belle ardeur est de courte durée. Papa n'a pas que ça à faire, et les manuels se montrent revêches. Il renonce. Les enfants prennent alors l'ordinateur en main (60% des utilisateurs ont moins de 25 ans, et parmi eux plus de la moitié ont moins de 15 ans). Ils veulent surtout s'amuser avec les logiciels qu'ils ont déjà vus dans les salles de jeux ou chez des amis. (Les programmes ludiques forment 55% des programmes vendus alors que les programmes utilitaires n'en composent que 12%). Ils piratent des cassettes ou des disquettes chez les copains (57%), inventent leurs propres programmes (71%), achètent de nouveaux logiciels (81%).

Cependant, au bout de trois mois, le clavier plastique et le petit téléviseur ont perdu de leur magie. Les parents coriaces, qui étaient restés dans le coup jusque-là, finissent par abandonner, ne laissant qu'un noyau de fidèles irréductibles.

Enfin, toujours selon cette enquête chiffrée, l'ordinateur en s'immisçant dans nos foyers en bouleverserait l'ambiance. Il serait le champion du rapprochement des générations (estiment 55% d'utilisateurs) et (pour 18% de sondés) un sacré semeur de zizanie entre mari et femme …

* Fédération nationale d'achats des cadres

A contemporary commentary on the early days of computers in the home, by Bernard Werber, writing in *Le Nouvel Observateur*, December 1985. © LE NOUVEL OBSERVATEUR

# Dad, the computer, and me

The profile of the average Homo informaticus is at last known. It is a small boy who has asked to be given an inexpensive micro-computer for Christmas and who taps away at it for fifty minutes a day, six days a month, in order to fight against crazed meteorites. These are, in substance, the conclusions reached by Fnac researchers who carried out a survey among their customers.

The figures revealed last week speak for themselves. Typical scenario: dad (90% of purchasers are men), influenced by his pals, decides to buy a micro-computer for his offspring. Dad is usually an executive with a university education. He barely hesitates, doesn't try it out and generally takes the least expensive one (for 67% of people the price is the most important criterion for choosing a computer, more important even than the amount of software available or ease of use). As soon as he arrives home, dad reads the instructions and announces to everyone that he has every intention of tackling BASIC (47% of purchasers want to learn to program before buying). But this great enthusiasm is of short duration. Dad has other things to do, and the handbooks turn out to be rather daunting. He gives up. The children then take over the computer (60% of users are aged under 25 and, of these, more than half are under 15). They particularly want to play with the software they have already seen in the amusement arcades or at friends' houses. (Computer games form 55% of all programs sold, whilst programs with a practical application account for only 12%). They pirate cassettes or diskettes at their friends' (57%), create their own programs (71%), buy new software (81%).

However, three months later, the plastic keyboard and the small television set have lost some of their magic. Persevering parents, who had participated in everything until then, finally give up, leaving just a small group of devoted enthusiasts.

Finally, again according to the statistics of this survey, it would seem that the computer, by intruding into our homes, upsets the atmosphere. Apparently, it is ideal for bringing the generations closer together (according to 55% of users) and (according to 18% of those interviewed) it is a constant source of friction [lit. 'a right sower of discord'] between husband and wife …

# Le retour du franc

Au secours, le franc revient! A moins de deux mois de son premier anniversaire, l'euro fiduciaire n'a pas encore trouvé sa place dans les têtes. Pis, il est en train de perdre à nouveau du terrain dans le coeur des consommateurs. Véritables étrangers dans leur propres pays, les Européens continuent massivement à raisonner dans leur ancienne monnaie ...

Depuis la rentrée, on voit ressurgir sur les étiquettes, mais aussi dans les publicités, les catalogues et même certain spots publicitaires, des prix en francs affichés aussi gros que le prix en euros. De grands distributeurs continuent ou recommencent à calculer les effets de seuil et les prix psychologiques en francs. 'La ménagère n'a aucune idée si elle fait une bonne affaire en achetant un produit à 19.99 euros. En revanche, elle sait si les 131.19 francs correspondants sont un bon prix', observe un spécialiste. Dès lors, le commerçant a plutôt intérêt à lui faire une offre à 129.90 francs (19.80 euros), qui va immédiatement lui 'parler'.

On assiste ainsi à la mise en place d'un cercle vicieux: plus on prolonge, au nom du confort des consommateurs, l'usage des anciennes monnaies, plus on retarde l'entrée de l'euro dans le quotidien des Européens. Les Français, dit-on, déjà peu doués pour le calcul mental, seraient plus mal lotis que les autres Européens, en raison du taux de conversion plus compliqué à mettre en oeuvre, un euro valant 6,55957 francs. Les Allemands, avec une parité de quasiment un euro pour deux marks, seraient plus à l'aise. Idée fausse: selon un sondage réalisé en octobre pour RTL Télévision, outre-Rhin, 80% des consommateurs comptent encore en marks, pourtant rayés des étiquettes depuis mars.

Une chose est sûre: si le passage à l'euro a été facteur d'inflation pour les prix, la persistance ou le retour au franc ne se traduira pas par des baisses ...

By Pascal Galinier, writing in *Le Monde Argent*, November 2002. © LE MONDE

# The return of the franc

Help, the franc is coming back! Less than two months before its first anniversary, the euro currency [literally 'the fiduciary euro'] has not yet found its place in people's heads. Worse, it is again losing ground in consumers' hearts. Actual foreigners in their own countries, Europeans continue overwhelmingly to think in their old currencies ...

Since 'la rentrée' [the return from the summer holidays], we have seen reappear not only on price labels, but also in advertisements, catalogues, and even TV commercials, prices in francs displayed as large as the price in euros. Major distributors are continuing, or beginning again, to calculate threshold prices and psychological prices in francs. 'The housewife has no idea whether she is getting a bargain when she buys a product for 19.99 euros. On the other hand, she knows whether the equivalent 131.19 francs is a good price,' an expert observes. Consequently, it is definitely in the shopkeeper's interest to make her an offer at 129.90 francs (19.80 euros), which will immediately mean something to her [literally 'speak to her'].

So we are witnessing the setting up of a vicious circle: the more we continue using the old currency, for the convenience of consumers, the more we are delaying the entry of the euro into Europeans' everyday lives. The French, already not very gifted for mental arithmetic, it is believed, are supposed to be worse off than the other Europeans, due to the more complicated conversion rate to be implemented, with one euro worth 6.559578 francs. The Germans, with a parity of roughly one euro to two marks, are said to be more comfortable. Wrong: according to a poll carried out in October for RTL Television on the other side of the Rhine, 80% of consumers still count in marks, although these have been removed from price labels since March.

One thing is certain: if the change to the euro played a role [literally 'was a factor'] in price inflation, the continued use [literally 'persistence'] or return of the franc will not translate into a drop in prices ...

# Key to exercises

## Week 1

**Exercise 1:** 1 le passeport. 2 l'hôtel. 3 la valise. 4 une station. 5 une leçon. 6 un chéquier. 7 une personne. 8 les journalistes. 9 les prix. 10 de la bière. 11 du vin. 12 des lettres. 13 des journaux. 14 des autobus.

**Exercise 2:** 1 Oui, elle a un journal. 2 Oui, ils ont une voiture. 3 Oui, j'ai une radio. 4 Oui, j'ai une carte. 5 Oui, nous avons une clé. 6 Oui, vous avez un CD.

**Exercise 3:** 1 Non, je n'ai pas de valise. 2 Non, je n'ai pas de passeport. 3 Non, nous n'avons pas de vin. 4 Non, nous n'avons pas de livre. 5 Non, il n'a pas de CD. 6 Non, elle n'a pas de radio. 7 Non, vous n'avez pas de journaux. 8 Non, elles n'ont pas d'appareil-photo.

**Exercise 4:** 1 J'ai une voiture. 2 Je n'ai pas de clés. 3 Nous avons une valise. 4 Elle a de l'alcool. 5 Il n'a pas de journal. 6 Ils ont des livres. 7 Elles n'ont pas de cartes. 8 Vous n'avez pas de chéquier. 9 Vous avez un appareil-photo? 10 Vous avez des CD? 11 Vous avez des livres? 12 Vous avez une radio?

## Week 2

**Exercise 5:** 1 Je suis médecin. 2 Il est pilote. 3 Elle est journaliste. 4 Nous sommes banquiers. 5 Vous êtes avocat. 6 Elles sont professeurs. 7 Ils sont astronautes.

**Exercise 6:** 1 Le banquier est pauvre. 2 La secrétaire est stupide. 3 Les médecins sont malheureux. 4 Les journaux sont ennuyeux. 5 Le vin est mauvais. 6 Le livre est difficile. 7 L'avocate est impolie. 8 La bière est bonne.

**Exercise 7:** 1 Nous habitons à Versailles. 2 Elle travaille à Nice. 3 Il voyage. 4 Je parle deux langues. 5 Elles pratiquent un sport. 6 Ils regardent la télévision. 7 Vous écoutez la radio. 8 Nous préparons une enquête.

**Exercise 8:** 1 Est-ce que vous téléphonez à l'hôtel? 2 Est-ce que vous réservez une chambre? 3 Est-ce que vous invitez le directeur à dîner? 4 Elle est intelligente? 5 Elle est intéressante? 6 Elle est grande? 7 Exporte-t-il des ordinateurs en France? 8 Importe-t-il des voitures? 9 Vote-t-il pour le président?

**Exercise 9:** a) neuf. b) deux. c) douze. d) cinq. e) quinze. f) douze. g) quatorze. h) trois.

## Week 3

**Exercise 10:** 1 Je finis le rapport. 2 Nous garantissons le magnétoscope. 3 Elle choisit un gâteau. 4 Il grossit. 5 Elles maigrissent. 6 Ils remplissent les verres. 7 Nous saisissons l'occasion.

**Exercise 11:** 1 Ce train est rapide. 2 Cette gare est importante. 3 Ce guichet est fermé. 4 Cette voiture est chère. 5 Cet ascenseur est plein. 6 Ces places sont réservées. 7 Ces compartiments sont occupés. 8 Ces billets sont valables.

**Exercise 12:** 1 Il a tort. 2 Elle a froid. 3 Ils ont raison. 4 Elles ont chaud.

**Exercise 13:** 1 Non, je ne travaille pas. 2 Non, je n'écoute pas. 3 Non, je n'ai pas faim. 4 Non, je ne choisis jamais de fromage. 5 Non, je ne téléphone jamais. 6 Non, je n'ai jamais froid. 7 Non, il ne mange rien. 8 Non, elle ne prépare rien. 9 Non, il n'exporte rien. 10 Non, nous n'invitons personne. 11 Non, nous ne choisissons personne. 12 Non, nous ne rencontrons personne. 13 Non, ils n'ont plus de voiture. 14 Non, elles n'habitent plus à Paris. 15 Non, elles ne travaillent plus.

**Exercise 14:** 1 Où travaillez-vous? 2 Quand regardez-vous le film? 3 Comment allez-vous? 4 Qui téléphone? 5 Qui cherchent-ils? 6 Pourquoi mangez-vous? 7 Quelles langues parlez-vous? 8 Combien de CD avez-vous? 9 Combien coûte ce journal? 10 Qu'est-ce que vous exportez?

**Exercise 15:** 1 Réservez deux chambres. 2 Cherchez François. 3 Saisissez l'occasion. 4 Choisissez la méthode Hugo. 5 Montez les bagages. 6 Ne mangez pas trop. 7 Ne grossissez pas. 8 Ne fumez pas. 9 Parlons français. 10 Écoutons la radio. 11 Finissons le rapport.

## Week 4

**Exercise 16:** 1 J'ai habité en France. 2 J'ai travaillé en Italie. 3 J'ai réservé les chambres. 4 Elle a écouté la radio. 5 Elle a regardé la télévision. 6 Elle a préparé le rapport. 7 Il a grossi. 8 Il a choisi le fromage. 9 Il a fini le livre. 10 Nous avons copié le document. 11 Nous avons acheté la voiture. 12 Nous avons téléphoné. 13 Vous avez garanti la platine laser. 14 Vous avez saisi l'occasion. 15 Vous avez invité le président. 16 Ils ont maigri. 17 Elles ont dépensé 15 euros. 18 Elles ont traversé la Manche.

**Exercise 17:** 1 Non, je n'ai pas réservé la chambre. 2 Non, je n'ai pas écouté le CD. 3 Non, il n'a pas regardé le film. 4 Non, elle n'a pas préparé le document. 5 Non, nous n'avons pas fini. 6 Non, ils n'ont pas choisi. 7 Non, elles n'ont pas mangé.

**Exercise 18:** 1 Votre premier vol. 2 Attachez votre ceinture de sécurité. 3 Où sont nos billets? 4 Voici son passeport. 5 Voici sa place. 6 Leurs valises sont dans l'avion. 7 Où sont mes journaux?

**Exercise 19:** 1 C'est ennuyeux. 2 C'est mauvais. 3 C'est impossible. 4 C'est difficile. 5 C'est affreux. 6 C'est tôt.

**Exercise 20:** 1 Il est deux heures et quart. 2 Il est quatre heures et demie. 3 Il est six heures. 4 Il est huit heures vingt. 5 Le train arrive à dix heures et quart. 6 Le car arrive à midi moins le quart (or minuit moins le quart). 7 Le bateau part à midi vingt-cinq. 8 L'aéroglisseur part à une heure moins le quart. 9 Le président arrive à neuf heures et quart. 10 La conférence de presse est à dix heures et quart.

**Exercise 21:** 1 Le premier janvier. 2 Le premier mai.
3 Le quatorze juillet. 4 Le vingt-cinq décembre. 5 Le onze
novembre. 6 Le vingt et un mars.

**Exercise 22:** 1 J'ai travaillé lundi. 2 J'ai écouté la radio
mardi. 3 J'ai regardé la télévision mercredi. 4 J'ai fini le
rapport jeudi. 5 J'ai acheté un livre vendredi. 6 J'ai
téléphoné à ma femme samedi. 7 J'ai parlé espagnol
dimanche. 8 Je travaille le lundi. 9 Elle écoute la radio le
mardi. 10 Nous regardons la télévision le mercredi.

## Self-assessment test 1

**A:** 1 le médecin. 2 l'ordinateur. 3 du vin. 4 de la bière.
5 ma voiture. 6 mes clés. 7 ce train. 8 ces journaux.

**B:** 1 riche. 2 heureux. 3 ennuyeux. 4 affreux. 5 difficile.

**C:** 1 regarder. 2 écouter. 3 choisir. 4 pratiquer. 5 attacher.
6 réserver. 7 voyager. 8 saisir. 9 consulter. 10 traverser.

**D:** 1 six heures et quart. 2 neuf heures moins le quart.
3 dix heures vingt. 4 midi/minuit moins le quart.

**E:** 1 mercredi. 2 dimanche. 3 vendredi. 4 mardi.

**F:** Jeudi means 'on Thursday'; le jeudi means 'on
Thursdays', 'every Thursday'.

**G:** 1 le deux février. 2 le cinq avril. 3 le douze juin.
4 le trente et un août.

**H:** 1 Non, j'ai réservé les chambres lundi. 2 Non, il a fini le
livre lundi. 3 Non, elle a copié le document lundi. 4 Non,
ils ont téléphoné lundi.

**I:** 1 Je n'ai pas fini le rapport. 2 Elle n'a pas téléphoné à son
mari samedi. 3 Nous n'avons pas visité l'Italie. 4 Ils n'ont
pas maigri.

**J:** a) vingt-neuf. b) trente-six. c) quarante-cinq. d) trente et un. e) quarante-quatre. f) cinquante. g) quinze. h) soixante-deux. i) seize.

**K:** avoir

**L:** Nous désirons passer deux semaines en France au printemps. Nous avons visité l'Italie en août, mais nous avons trouvé la chaleur insupportable. • Non, par le train, c'est plus agréable. • Oui, d'accord. Départ neuf avril, retour vingt-trois avril.

**Score:**

| | | |
|---|---|---|
| 80–100% | = | excellent. |
| 60–79% | = | good/very good. Progressing well. |
| 45–59% | = | satisfactory – but you should devote more time to your studies. |
| Below 45% | = | serious revision needed. |

## Week 5

**Exercise 23:** 1 Je vends ma voiture. 2 Il attend sa femme. 3 Nous rendons soixante francs. 4 Cela dépend de mes parents. 5 Est-ce qu'elles entendent la musique? 6 Elle a vendu sa maison. 7 Nous n'avons pas répondu. 8 Avez-vous descendu les bagages? 9 Attends-tu ton frère? 10 As-tu perdu ta mère?

**Exercise 24:** 1 Est-ce que vous avez pris le train? 2 J'ai appris le français. 3 Apprenez-vous la langue? 4 Comprenez-vous? 5 Tu as souvent surpris ton professeur?

**Exercise 25:** 1 J'ai mis une annonce dans le journal. 2 Il a permis à sa secrétaire de partir tôt. 3 Vous avez promis de répondre à la lettre? 4 Elle a soumis le rapport ce matin. 5 Mettez-vous le dictionnaire dans la valise? 6 Permettent-ils à leurs enfants de rentrer tard? 7 Nous promettons de parler français. 8 Soumettez-vous déjà le projet?

**Exercise 26:** 1 rapidement. 2 facilement. 3 finalement.
4 heureusement. 5 attentivement. 6 lentement.
7 complètement. 8 normalement. 9 principalement.
10 temporairement.

**Exercise 27:** 1 Le rapport? Il est très important. 2 La bière?
Elle est mauvaise. 3 La poche? Elle est pleine. 4 L'appareil?
Il est excellent. 5 Le restaurant? Il est fermé. 6 La qualité?
Elle est très bonne. 7 Les produits? Ils sont français. 8 Les
messages? Ils sont en anglais. 9 L'explication? Elle n'est pas
claire. 10 Le répondeur automatique? Il n'est pas cher.

**Exercise 28:** 1 Oui, elle vous cherche. 2 Oui, elle me consulte. 3 Oui, je le rencontre. 4 Oui, je la copie. 5 Oui, il
l'invite. 6 Oui, il les exporte. 7 Oui, nous le comprenons.
8 Oui, nous la branchons. 9 Oui, nous le mettons en
marche. 10 Oui, nous le copions. 11 Oui, elles nous
répondent en français . 12 Oui, ils lui téléphonent . 13 Oui,
ils lui téléphonent. 14 Oui, ils leur téléphonent. 15 Oui, je
lui parle. 16 Oui, je leur réponds. 17 Oui, je leur défends
de rentrer tard.

**Exercise 29:** 1 Oui, je l'ai invité. 2 Oui, je l'ai invitée.
3 Oui, je les ai invités. 4 Oui, il les a exportées. 5 Oui, elle
l'a consulté. 6 Oui, elle l'a consultée. 7 Oui, elle les a con-
sultés. 8 Oui, ils l'ont branchée. 9 Oui, ils les ont réservées.
10 Oui, ils l'ont perdue. 11 Oui, nous l'avons compris.
12 Oui, nous l'avons comprise. 13 Oui, nous les avons
comprises. 14 Oui, nous les avons compris. 15 Oui, je l'ai
mis dans ma poche.

## Week 6

**Exercise 30:** 1 Il y a une serviette sur la table. 2 Il y a un
taxi devant l'hôtel. 3 Il y a un restaurant derrière l'église.
4 Il y a un supermarché à côté de la banque. 5 Il y a une
librairie en face de l'université. 6 Est-ce qu'il y a une cabine
téléphonique près de la gare? 7 Est-ce qu'il y a des livres
anglais à la bibliothèque? 8 Est-ce qu'il y a un tunnel sous
la Manche? 9 Je vais au cinéma. 10 Elle va aux États-Unis.

11 Avez-vous le numéro de téléphone du théâtre? 12 J'ai acheté un journal pour mon ami(e). 13 Elle apprend le français avec des CD. 14 C'est difficile de travailler sans ma secrétaire. 15 Mangeons après le spectacle. 16 Téléphonons avant 9 heures.

**Exercise 31:** 1 Le banquier est plus riche que le professeur. 2 Le facteur est plus pauvre que l'avocat. 3 Le pilote est aussi courageux que l'astronaute. 4 Le français n'est pas si difficile que le russe. 5 Elle parle plus distinctement que Paul. 6 Il écoute plus attentivement que son frère.

**Exercise 32:** 1 Oui, c'est le restaurant le plus chic du monde. 2 Oui, c'est la plus grande librairie du monde. 3 Oui, c'est le magasin le plus célèbre du monde. 4 Oui, c'est la plus belle cathédrale du monde. 5 Oui, c'est la meilleure bière du monde. 6 Oui, c'est le parc le plus agréable du monde. 7 Oui, c'est la ville la plus intéressante du monde. 8 Oui, c'est la voiture la plus confortable du monde. 9 Oui, c'est l'avion le plus impressionnant du monde.

**Exercise 33:** 1 Il pleut. 2 Il fait du brouillard. 3 Il fait du vent. 4 Il fait froid. 5 Il fait du soleil. 6 Il neige. 7 Il fait chaud. 8 Il fait mauvais. 9 Il fait beau.

**Exercise 34:** A. 1 Je suis médecin. 2 Ce matin je suis arrivé à l'hôpital à 7 heures. 3 Je suis allé à une réunion à 10 heures. 4 Je suis parti avec deux infirmières. B. 1 Je suis journaliste. 2 Hier je suis allée à une conférence de presse. 3 Je suis montée au restaurant à une heure. 4 Je suis retournée au bureau très tard. C. 1 Nicole et Sophie sont étudiantes. 2 Ce matin elles sont allées à l'université à 9 heures. 3 Elles sont restées toute la journée à la bibliothèque. 4 Elles sont revenues à la maison à 5 heures.

**Exercise 35:** 1 Les ingénieurs sont arrivés hier. 2 Les infirmières sont déjà parties. 3 Nous sommes revenues tôt. 4 Tu es descendu. 5 Est-ce que le docteur est resté toute la journée? 6 Etes-vous revenu très tard?

**Exercise 36:** 1 Je voudrais une carte postale. 2 Je voudrais un timbre. 3 Je voudrais un plan de la ville. 4 Je voudrais un journal américain. 5 Je voudrais du lait. 6 Je voudrais du sucre. 7 Je voudrais du thé. 8 Je voudrais téléphoner à New York. 9 Je voudrais régler la note.

**Exercise 37:** 1 Il me faut un crayon. 2 Il me faut un stylo-bille. 3 Il lui faut une gomme. 4 Il lui faut du papier à lettres. 5 Il leur faut des enveloppes. 6 Il leur faut des cigarettes. 7 Il leur faut des allumettes.

## Week 7

**Exercise 38:** 1 Non, j'ai beaucoup de cravates. 2 Non, j'ai beaucoup de costumes. 3 Non, j'ai beaucoup de robes. 4 Oui, il a maintenant trop de pantalons. 5 Oui, elle a maintenant trop de jupes. 6 Oui, elle a maintenant trop de foulards. 7 Il a peu de patience. 8 Avez-vous (or as-tu) mis assez de chemises dans la valise? 9 J'ai plus de cardigans que Monique. 10 Vous avez moins de costumes que Pierre.

**Exercise 39:** 1 Je vais écouter la radio. 2 Je vais acheter un journal. 3 Je vais étudier le français. 4 Je vais faire mes courses. 5 Il réparera la voiture. 6 Il jouera au tennis. 7 Il écrira une lettre. 8 Il visitera le musée. 9 Ils tapisseront l'appartement. 10 Ils organiseront une réunion. 11 Ils iront à une conférence internationale. 12 Ils passeront un week-end à Londres. 13 Elle finira sa lettre. 14 Nous irons au théâtre la semaine prochaine. 15 Vous surprendrez votre père. 16 Tu choisiras ta robe le mois prochain.

**Exercise 40:** 1 Je peux acheter les légumes au marché. 2 Je peux préparer le rapport. 3 Nous ne pouvons pas arriver lundi. 4 Nous ne pouvons pas lire son écriture. 5 Elle doit signer le contrat. 6 Elle doit arrêter de fumer. 7 Ils ne doivent pas décourager les étudiants. 8 Ils ne doivent pas garer la voiture devant l'hôpital. 9 Il veut faire le tour du monde. 10 Il veut dépenser moins d'argent. 11 Savez-vous (or sais-tu) conduire? 12 Savez-vous (or sais-tu) nager?

**Exercise 41:** Check your list of countries against the lists in section 49.

**Exercise 42:** 1 Nous passons nos vacances en Grèce.
2 Avez-vous l'intention d'aller au Japon? 3 L'Allemagne exporte des voitures en France. 4 Est-ce que le diplomate est arrivé en Russie?

**Exercise 43:** a) Vingt. b) Vingt-deux. c) Trente et un.
d) Quarante-sept. e) Cinquante-neuf. f) Soixante et un.
g) Soixante-dix. h) Soixante-dix-neuf. i) Quatre-vingt-un.
j) Quatre-vingt-onze. k) Quatre-vingt-dix-neuf. l) Cent.

## Week 8

**Exercise 44:** 1 Il jouait au football. 2 Il allait à la pêche.
3 Il collectionnait des timbres. 4 Elle chantait. 5 Elle écoutait des disques. 6 Nous apprenions l'espagnol. 7 Nous habitions dans une petite maison. 8 Nous faisions de la photo(graphie). 9 Je finissais la traduction quand j'ai entendu un bruit en haut. 10 Elle faisait les courses quand elle a perdu son porte-monnaie. 11 Ils regardaient la télévision quand le cambrioleur est entré dans la maison.

**Exercise 45:** 1 L'hôtel, que vous cherchez, est à droite. 2 Je voudrais la chambre qui donne sur le parc. 3 La chambre, que nous avons réservée pour vous, est à côté de l'ascenseur. 4 J'ai apporté le petit déjeuner que votre mari a commandé. 5 Où est le poste de télévision qui ne marche pas? 6 Les valises, qui sont dans le vestibule, sont très lourdes. 7 La réceptionniste, à qui vous avez parlé, est bilingue. 8 Le client, dont le fils est malade, est dans la chambre 5. 9 N'avez-vous pas compris ce que la femme de chambre vous a dit? 10 La note, que vous avez préparée, est correcte.

**Exercise 46:** 1 Si j'étais riche, je ferais le tour du monde.
2 Si je ne travaillais pas, je peindrais et je dessinerais.
3 S'il avait beaucoup de temps, il apprendrait le portugais.
4 Si elle parlait français, elle travaillerait comme interprète.
5 Si elle parlait allemand, elle travaillerait comme secrétaire

bilingue. 6 Si vous étiez marié, vous rentreriez plus tôt le soir à la maison. 7 S'ils étaient en chômage, ils chercheraient du travail. 8 Si elles avaient des enfants, elles resteraient à la maison. 9 Si j'avais le temps, je lirais beaucoup. 10 Si nous voulions maigrir, nous mangerions moins et ferions de la gymnastique.

**Exercise 47:** 1 … avec lui. 2 … à côté d'elle. 3 … sans eux. 4 … qu'elles. 5 … que lui. 6 … Elle. 7 Ce sont (or C'est) eux qui …

**Exercise 48:** 1 Je ne sais pas si Paul a fini son travail. 2 Je ne connais pas les Dupont. 3 Savez-vous où je peux louer un ordinateur? 4 Savez-vous si le médecin est libre? 5 Est-ce que Marie-Claude connaît ma tante?

**Exercise 49:** 1 Je ne vous dérange pas. Je pensais justement à vous. Vous n'êtes pas trop occupée? . . . quand vous avez frappé à la porte. À qui est-ce que vous écriviez? À propos, comment va votre travail? Qu'est-ce que vous feriez de tout ce temps libre? Vous feriez mieux de prendre votre retraite tout de suite.

## Self-assessment test 2

**A:** 1 devant. 2 à côté de. 3 en face de. 4 sous. 5 près de. 6 sans. 7 après. 8 avant.

**B:** 1 Je suis journaliste. 2 Ce matin, je suis arrivé(e) à l'hôtel à sept heures. 3 Je suis allé(e) à une conférence internationale à dix heures. 4 Je suis parti(e) très tard.

**C:** 1 Il pleut. 2 Il fait chaud. / Il fait du soleil. 3 Il fait/Il y a du brouillard. 4 Il fait froid. / Il neige. 5 Il fait froid. / Il fait du vent.

**D:** 1 le Portugal. 2 le Japon. 3 les États-Unis. 4 la Grèce. 5 l'Espagne. 6 l'Italie. 7 la Hollande / les Pays-Bas. 8 la Chine. 9 la Belgique. 10 la France. 11 l'Angleterre. 12 le Danemark.

**E:** a) cinquante-huit. b) soixante-dix. c) soixante-quinze. d) quatre-vingt-trois. e) quatre-vingt-dix. f) quatre-vingt-dix-neuf. g) cent.

**F:** 1 Il jouait au football. 2 Elle apprenait l'anglais. 3 Ils habitaient dans une grande maison. 4 Ils faisaient les courses quand elle a perdu son porte-monnaie.

**G:** 1 Si j'étais riche, je visiterais le Japon et la Chine. 2 Si elle parlait italien, elle travaillerait comme secrétaire bilingue. 3 Si tu étais au chômage, tu chercherais du travail. 4 Si nous avions beaucoup de temps, nous lirions beaucoup.

**H:** a) Savoir means 'to know a fact'. Connaître is used with the meaning of 'to be acquainted with' (persons, places etc). b) Je ne sais pas jouer ... means 'I do not know how to ...'; je ne peux pas jouer ... means something (such as a broken finger) prevents me from playing.

**I:** • J'ai décidé de changer ma vie. Je vais regarder la télévision moins souvent. Je mangerai plus de fruits. Je ferai de la gymnastique chaque matin. Je dépenserai moins d'argent en vêtements. • Oui, j'aurai plus de temps et plus d'argent, et je serai en meilleure santé.

### Score

| | | |
|---|---|---|
| 80–100% | = | excellent. You've done really well! |
| 60–79% | = | very good. |
| 45–59% | = | satisfactory – try to find time to study a little every day. |
| Below 45% | = | you must revise. It's important to consolidate your knowledge before going on. |

## Week 9

**Exercise 50:** 1 Mon rhume est pire que celui de ma soeur. 2 Cet hôpital est plus moderne que celui que la Princesse a visité l'année dernière. 3 Quel chirurgien a effectué la greffe du coeur? Celui-ci ou celui-là? 4 Avez-vous rendez-vous (or un rendez-vous) avec ce dentiste-ci ou celui-là? 5 Le (la) kinésithérapeute m'a donné ceci. 6 Le pharmacien a préparé cela. 7 C'est votre nouvelle secrétaire. 8 Ce sont vos malades.

**Exercise 51:** 1 Le barman vous a servi votre whisky, mais où est le mien? 2 Mon poisson est délicieux; le vôtre n'est pas frais. 3 J'ai payé notre addition et ils ont payé la leur. 4 Est-ce que ce chapeau est à vous ou à votre ami? 5 Avec quoi voulez-vous manger ce repas chinois? Avec des baguettes? Quoi? Non! Avec un couteau et une fourchette. 6 Quel est le numéro de téléphone du restaurant italien? 7 Quels légumes a-t-elle commandés? 8 Qu'est-ce qui sent si bon? 9 Voici une liste des meilleurs restaurants de Paris; lequel préférez-vous? 10 A qui est cette cuillère?

**Exercise 52:** 1 Ils chantent mal. 2 Ne parlez pas si bas. 3 Il va souvent chez ses parents. 4 Nous avons déjà mangé. 5 Il va sûrement pleuvoir ou neiger. 6 Elle prend un bain en bas. 7 Elles ont fait les courses hier.

## Week 10

**Exercise 53:** 1 Il se réveille à 7 heures du matin. 2 Il se lave. 3 Il se rase. 4 Il va au travail. 5 Elle se lève à 8 heures du matin. 6 Elle prend une douche. 7 Elle se peigne. 8 Elle se maquille. 9 Elle va à la gare. 10 Nous nous lavons. 11 Nous nous habillons vite. 12 Nous nous promenons. 13 Nous nous couchons à dix heures du soir. 14 Je me suis amusée. 15 Vous ne vous êtes pas trompée. 16 Elles se reposent. 17 Ils ont lavé la voiture eux-mêmes. 18 Nous nous brossons les dents chaque matin.

**Exercise 54:** 1 Il a quitté la maison sans dire un mot. 2 Elle est habituée à écouter la radio dans sa chambre. 3 Avant de réparer la lampe, il a téléphoné à l'électricien. 4 Après avoir préparé le petit déjeuner, il a fait le ménage. 5 Ma mère a commencé par dire que toute la famille était en bonne santé et a fini par souhaiter à tout le monde une bonne année. 6 Ces CD sont excellents pour apprendre le français.

**Exercise 55:** 1 J'ai l'intention d'acheter des lunettes de soleil. 2 Sera-t-il possible de faire des excursions? 3 Nous préférons louer un appartement. 4 Ils m'ont invitée à aller à la pêche. 5 J'hésite à faire du ski nautique. 6 Aurez-vous l'occasion de faire de la planche à voile?

**Exercise 56:** 1 Est-ce-que vous me l'avez donné? 2 Il nous les a promises. 3 Il a l'intention de me les vendre. 4 Je le lui ai envoyé. 5 Il la lui montre. 6 Nous les leur avons données.

## Week 11

**Exercise 57:** 1 Puisque (or comme) l'ami de Paul vient camper avec nous, nous devrons acheter un sac de couchage supplémentaire. 2 Quand vous saurez parler français, nous irons faire du camping en France. 3 Saisissez-vous chaque occasion pour parler français, quand vous êtes en Belgique? 4 Je n'aime pas ce camping parce qu'il n'y a pas de piscine. 5 Nous sommes quatre mais nous avons seulement (or nous n'avons que) trois sacs de couchage. 6 La voiture est tombée en panne, donc nous avons décidé de camper dans un champ.

**Exercise 58:** a) deux cent cinquante. b) trois cents. c) quatre cent trente. d) cinq cent soixante-dix. e) six cent quatre-vingts. f) mille quatre cent quarante.

**Exercise 59:** 1 la première discothèque. 2 le deuxième (second) casino. 3 la troisième boîte de nuit. 4 le quatrième théâtre. 5 le cinquième concert. 6 le sixième opéra. 7 le septième cinéma. 8 la huitième patinoire. 9 le neuvième ballet. 10 le dixième restaurant.

**Exercise 60:** 1 L'importance de la décision a été soulignée par le président de la République française. 2 La Grande-Bretagne sera reliée au continent par un tunnel ferroviaire en 1993. 3 Un lien routier sera construit plus tard. 4 Cette décision historique a été annoncée à Lille. 5 Les touristes étrangers ont souvent été découragés par la traversée de la Manche.

**Exercise 61:** 1 Elle s'est cassé le bras en faisant du ski. 2 Je suis tombé en patinant. 3 En allant aux cours du soir trois fois par semaine, il a obtenu son diplôme. 4 Voyant que l'automobiliste était blessé, l'agent de police a appelé une ambulance. 5 En téléphonant vous aurez la réponse tout de suite.

**Exercise 62:** 1 Téléphonez-lui – non, ne lui téléphonez pas. 2 Envoyez-leur cette brochure – non, ne la leur envoyez pas. 3 Copiez ce document – non, ne le copiez pas. 4 Donnez-moi le catalogue – non, ne me le donnez pas. 5 Envoyez-lui les échantillons – non, ne les lui envoyez pas. 6 Soyez ici à 9 heures – non, à 8 heures. 7 Voulez-vous bien faire des heures supplémentaires?

**Exercise 63:** 1 Je suis marié depuis cinq ans. 2 J'habite dans cette maison depuis quatre ans. 3 Je travaille pour cette banque depuis trois ans. 4 J'ai cette voiture depuis deux ans. 5 J'apprends à jouer du piano depuis un an.

**Exercise 64:** 1 Mais je viens d'appeler un docteur. 2 Mais je viens de prévenir les pompiers. 3 Mais je viens de vous montrer mon permis de conduire. 4 Mais les ambulanciers viennent de transporter les blessés à l'hôpital. 5 Mais je viens de vous donner mon adresse.

## Week 12

**Exercise 65:** 1 Qu'est-ce que vous faites dans la vie? 2 Ma soeur fait une tarte aux pommes. 3 Je vais faire une conférence sur la psychologie devant 200 personnes. 4 Elle a fait une promenade au parc hier. 5 Il fait de la fièvre. 6 Ne fais pas l'idiot. 7 J'ai fait travailler mon fils. 8 Je me fais construire une maison à Avignon.

**Exercise 66:** 1 he gave. 2 I sold. 3 we finished. 4 she had. 5 I was. 6 you had. 7 he took. 8 she went out. 9 they read. 10 they put.

**Exercise 67:** 1 Je suggère que le président fasse une déclaration à la télévision. 2 Il faut que nous continuions

notre conquête de l'espace. 3 Il voudrait que le lancement du vaisseau spatial ait lieu la semaine prochaine.
4 Je suis content que vous participiez à cette mission spatiale. 5 Il est important que le lancement soit filmé en direct. 6 A moins que vous ne puissiez me donner toutes les données enregistrées par les ordinateurs, je ne peux pas prendre de décision. 7 Nous sommes contents que le président ait décidé de reporter son discours. 8 Bien que les astronautes soient habitués à l'apesanteur, ils ont quand même un peu de mal à mener leurs expériences à bord du vaisseau spatial.

## Self-assessment test 3

**A:** 1 Je me réveille à huit heures du matin. 2 Je me lave. 3 Je me rase. 4 Je vais au travail. 5 Monique se lève à neuf heures. 6 Elle se lave. 7 Elle s'habille vite. 8 Elle va au bureau. 9 (Hier) Nicole et moi, nous nous sommes réveillées à dix heures. 10 Nous nous sommes maquillées. 11 Nous sommes allées à la gare.

**B:** 1 sans dire. 2 avant de répondre. 3 par critiquer. 4 Après avoir acheté.

**C:** car/parce que. 2 donc. 3 Pendant que. 4 mais. 5 Quand/ Aussitôt que.

**D:** a) quatre cent quarante. b) trois cents. c) sept cent quatre-vingts. d) trois cent dix. e) mille trois cent trente. f) cinq cents.

**E:** 1 Depuis quand es-tu en Angleterre? / Depuis combien de temps es-tu en Angleterre? 2 Je travaille ici depuis le deux mai. 3 Nous apprenons le français depuis trois mois. 4 Nous venons d'acheter un appartement. 5 Ils viennent d'appeler un médecin / docteur.

**F:** 1 Nous espérons aller à la plage. 2 Ils ont décidé de louer une voiture. 3 Elles sont contentes de voir le soleil. 4 Elle a l'intention d'acheter des lunetttes de soleil.

5 J'hésite à faire du ski nautique. 6 Auras-tu l'occasion de faire de la planche à voile?

**G:** 1 Qu'est-ce que vous faites dans la vie? 2 Ma mère fait un gâteau. 3 Je vais faire une conférence sur la conquête de l'espace devant cent personnes. 4 Il a fait une promenade au parc.

**H:** 1 Copiez-la – non, ne la copiez pas. 2 Envoyez-les – non, ne les envoyez pas. 3 Donnez-le-moi – non, ne me le donnez pas. 4 Téléphonez-leur – non, ne leur téléphonez pas.

**I:** 1 Je voudrais que vous fixiez un rendez-vous. 2 Je veux bien vous aider, à condition que vous finissiez le travail aujourd'hui. 3 Il est dommage que Sophie ne vienne pas à la réception. 4 Nous sommes contents qu'ils aient trouvé une petite maison.

**J:** • Oui, bien sûr. Je les ai achetés parce que je dois apprendre l'anglais en trois mois. • Oui, je les écoute le matin quand je me lave. Mon mari les écoute aussi, quand il se rase. Si je réussis à apprendre l'anglais, il me sera possible d'obtenir une promotion et de voyager aux États-Unis.

**Score:**

| | | |
|---|---|---|
| 80–100% | = | congratulations – you've made full use of this course! |
| 60–79% | = | well done! With a little revision you'll be able to improve your score. |
| 45–59% | = | satisfactory. Remember that the key to greater success is daily study and repetition. |
| Below 45% | = | much more revision needed; try writing out all the new words and expressions, as this helps to imprint them on your memory. |

# Mini-dictionary

This mini-dictionary contains the most important words found in the book plus a few others which you may find useful. See sections 23–26 for seasons, months of the year, dates and days of the week.

**able, to be able** pouvoir
**above** au-dessus de
**abroad** à l'étranger
**actress** actrice
**address** adresse (f.)
**advance, in advance** à l'avance
**advertisement** annonce (f.)
**advertising** publicité (f.)
**advise** conseiller
**after** après
**afternoon** après-midi (m or f)
**afterwards** ensuite
**again** encore
**agency** agence (f.)
**ago** il y a
**agree: I agree** je suis d'accord
**AIDS** sida (m.)
**air-conditioning** climatisation (f.)
**airline company** compagnie (f.) aérienne
**alcohol** alcool (m.)
**all** tout
**allow** permettre (irreg.)
**already** déjà
**also** aussi
**although** bien que, quoique
**always** toujours
**ambulance** ambulance (f.)
**ambulance driver** ambulancier (m.), -ière (f.)
**America** Amérique (f.)
**American** américain, Américain (m.), -e (f.)
**analyse** analyser
**and** et
**announce** annoncer
**answer (vb.)** répondre

**antique dealer** antiquaire (m. & f.)
**apple** pomme (f.)
**appointment** rendez-vous (m.)
**appreciate** apprécier
**approve (of)** approuver
**arm** bras (m.)
**armchair** fauteuil (m.)
**arrive** arriver
**ask (for)** demander
**astronaut** astronaute (m & f.)
**attach** attacher
**aunt** tante
**avoid** éviter

**bad** mauvais
**badly** mal
**bag** sac (m.)
  **handbag** sac à main
**baker's** boulangerie (f.)
**ball-point pen** stylo-bille (m.)
**bank** banque (f.)
**banker** banquier (m.)
**bar** bar (m.)
**bath** bain (m.)
**be, to be** être (irreg.)
**beach** plage (f.)
**beautiful** beau
**because** parce que
**bed lit (m.)**
  **to go to bed** se coucher
**bedroom** chambre (f.)
**beer** bière (f.)
**before** avant
**begin** commencer
**behind** derrière
**Belgium** Belgique (f.)

**better** meilleur, mieux
**between** entre
**bicycle** bicyclette (f.), vélo (m.)
**big** grand
**bilingual** bilingue
**bill** addition, note (f.)
**blood pressure** tension (f.)
**blue** bleu
**boat** bateau (m.)
**book** livre (m.)
**book (vb.)** réserver
**bookshop** librairie (f.)
**boring** ennuyeux
  **to be bored** s'ennuyer
**boss** patron (m.),-onne (f.)
**bottle** bouteille (f.)
**brand** marque (f.)
**brave** courageux
**bread** pain (m.)
**break** (vb.) casser
**breakdown** panne (f.)
**break down** tomber en panne
**breakfast** petit déjeuner (m.)
**briefcase** serviette (f.)
**bring** apporter, amener
**bring down** descendre
**bring up** monter
**Britain** Grande-Bretagne (f.)
**British** britannique
**broadcast** émission (f.)
**brochure** brochure (f.)
**brother** frère
**brown** brun
**build** construire (irreg.)
**burglar** cambrioleur (m.)
**burn (vb.)** brûler
**bus** autobus (m.)
**business** affaires (f. pl.)
**businessman** homme d'affaires
**busy** occupé
**but** mais
**butcher's** boucherie (f.)
**buy** acheter

**cake** gâteau (m.)
**call (vb.)** appeler
  **to be called** s'appeler
**camera** appareil-photo (m.)
**camp** (vb.) camper
**can (to be able)** pouvoir (irreg.)
**Canada** Canada (m.)
**cancel** annuler
**car** voiture (f.)
**card** carte (f.)
**cash: to pay in cash** payer en espèces
**cashdesk** caisse (f.)
**castle** château (m.)
**cathedral** cathédrale (f.)
**CD** CD (m.)
**CD player** platine laser (f.)
**chambermaid** femme de chambre
**change (vb.)** changer
**Channel** Manche (f.)
**check (vb.)** vérifier
**cheese** fromage (m.)
**chemist's** pharmacie (f.)
**cheque** chèque (m.)
**China** Chine (f.)
**Chinese** chinois, Chinois (m.) -e (f.)
**choose** choisir
**church** église (f.)
**clean (vb.)** nettoyer
**client** client (m.), -e (f.)
**close (vb.)** fermer
**clothes** vêtements (m. pl.)
**coach** car (m.)
**coffee** café (m.)
**cold** froid
  **to be cold** avoir froid
  **to have a cold** avoir un rhume
**colour** couleur (f.)
**come** venir (irreg.)
**comfortable** confortable
**complaint** plainte (f.)
**computer** ordinateur (m.)
  **(computer) software** logiciel (m.)
**conference** conférence (f.)
**confirm** confirmer
**congratulate** féliciter

**consult** consulter
**continue** continuer
**contract** contrat (m.)
**copy (vb.)** copier
**correct (vb.)** corriger
**cost (vb.)** coûter
**country** pays (m.)
**create** créer
**credit card** carte (f.) de crédit
**criticise** critiquer
**cross (vb.)** traverser
**cup** tasse (f.)
**customs** douane (f.)
**cut (vb.)** couper

**dance (vb.)** danser
**dangerous** dangereux
**date** date (f.); rendez-vous (m.)
**daughter** fille
**dear** cher
**decide** décider
**deckchair** chaise (f.) longue
**deep** profond
**degree (univ.)** licence (f.)
**delicious** délicieux
**dentist** dentiste (m. & f.)
**departure** départ (m.)
**deposit: to leave a deposit**
   verser des arrhes (f. pl.)
**dial (vb.)** composer
   (un numéro)
**dictionary** dictionnaire (m.)
**diet** régime (m.)
**difficult** difficile
**dinner** dîner (m.)
**director** directeur (m.), -trice (f.)
**dirty** sale
**disco** discothèque (f.)
**discourage** décourager
**discuss** discuter de
**disease** maladie (f.)
   **'mad cow' disease** maladie de
      la 'vache folle'
**disembark** débarquer
**dish** plat (m.)
**disturb** déranger

**dive (vb.)** plonger
**do** faire (irreg.)
**doctor** médecin, docteur (m.)
**doubt (vb.)** douter
**downstairs** en bas
**dreadful** affreux
**dress** robe (f.)
**drink (vb.)** boire (irreg.)
**drive (vb.)** conduire (irreg.),
   rouler
**driving licence** permis (m.)
   de conduire

**each** chaque
**early** tôt
**earn** gagner
**east** est (m.)
**easy** facile
**eat** manger
**efficient** efficace
**electrician** électricien (m.)
**embassy** ambassade (f.)
**emergency: in an emergency**
   en cas d'urgence
**encourage** encourager
**end** fin (f.)
**engine** moteur (m.)
**engineer** ingénieur (m.)
**England** Angleterre (f.)
**English** anglais
**enjoy oneself** s'amuser
**enough** assez
**enter** entrer
**entertainment** distractions (f. pl.)
**envelope** enveloppe (f.)
**especially** surtout
**euro** euro (m.)
**European Union** Union
   européenne
**even** même
**evening** soir (m.)
**everyone** tout le monde
**everything** tout
**everywhere** partout
**exactly** exactement
**excellent** excellent

**excursion** excursion (f.)
**expensive** cher
**explanation** explication (f.)
**export** exporter
**extra** supplément (m.)

**fall (vb.)** tomber
**family** famille (f.)
**famous** célèbre
**far** loin
**fashion** mode (f.)
**fast** rapide
**father** père
**fever** fièvre (f.)
**field** champ (m.)
**fill** remplir
**film** film (m.) (for snapshots) pellicule (f.)
**find** trouver
**fine beau;** bien
**finish (vb.)** finir
**fire** incendie (m.)
**fire exit** sortie (f.) de secours
**fireman** pompier
**first** premier
**fish** poisson (m.)
**fishing** pêche (f.)
  **to go fishing aller** à la pêche
**fishmonger's** poissonnerie (f.)
**flag** drapeau (m.)
**flat** appartement (m.)
**flight** vol (m.)
**fog** brouillard (m.)
**food** nourriture (f.)
**for** pour
**forbid** défendre
**foreign** étranger
**forget** oublier
**forgive** pardonner
**fork** fourchette (f.)
**fortunately** heureusement
**free** libre
**French** français
**fresh** frais, fraîche (f.)
**friend** ami (m.), -e (f.)
**from** de

**front: in front** of devant
**fruit** fruit(s) (m.)
**full** plein

**garage** garage (m.)
**garden** jardin (m.)
**generally** généralement
**German** allemand
**Germany** Allemagne (f.)
**get** obtenir (irreg.)
**get up** se lever
**gift** cadeau (m.)
**give** donner
**give back** rendre
**glad** content
**glass** verre (m.)
**glove** gant (m.)
**go** aller (irreg.)
**go down** descendre
**go out** sortir (irreg.)
**go up** monter
**good** bon, bonne (f.)
**goodbye** au revoir
**government** gouvernement (m.)
**Great Britain** Grande-Bretagne (f.)
**Greece** Grèce (f.)
**grey** gris
**group** groupe (m.)
**guarantee (vb.)** garantir
**guide** guide (m.)
**guide book** guide (m.)

**haggle** marchander
**hair** cheveux (m. pl.)
**hairdresser** coiffeur (m.), -euse (f.)
**half** moitié (f.)
**hall** vestibule (m.)
**ham** jambon (m.)
**hand** main (f.)
**handwriting** écriture (f.)
**happen** arriver, se passer
**happy** heureux
**harbour** port (m.)
**hat** chapeau (m.)
**hate (vb.)** détester
**have** avoir (irreg.)

**have to (must)** devoir (irreg.)
**hayfever** rhume (m.) des foins
**head** tête (f.)
**health** santé (f.)
**hear** entendre
**heart** coeur (m.)
**heavy** lourd
**help (vb.)** aider
**her** sa
**hers** sien (m.), sienne (f.)
**here** ici
**here is** voici
**hire** louer
**his** son
**holiday** vacances (f. pl.)
**hope (vb.)** espérer
**hospital** hôpital (m.)
**hot** chaud
**hotel** hôtel (m.)
**house** maison (f.)
**how** comment
**how much, how many** combien
**hungry: to be hungry** avoir faim
**hurry** se dépêcher
**husband** mari

**ice** glace (f.)
**ice cream** glace (f.)
**identification** pièce (f.) d'identité
**ill** malade
**immediately** tout de suite
**import** importer
**important** important
**impossible** impossible
**impressive** impressionnant
**improve** améliorer
**included** compris
**income** revenu (m.)
**increase (vb.)** augmenter
**increase** augmentation (f.)
**inexpensive** pas cher
**information** renseignement(s) (m.)
**injured** blessé
**interesting** intéressant
**interpreter** interprète (m. & f.)
**invite** inviter

**invoice** facture (f.)
**Ireland** Irlande (f.)
**Irish** irlandais

**jacket** veste (f.)
**jam** confiture (f.)
**Japan** Japon (m.)
**Japanese** japonais
**job** emploi (m.), poste (m.)
**journalist** journaliste (m. & f.)

**keep (vb.)** garder
**key** clé (f.)
**kind** aimable
**kitchen** cuisine (f.)
**knife** couteau (m.)
**knock (vb.)** frapper
**know** savoir (irreg.), connaître (irreg.)

**lady** dame
**lake** lac (m.)
**lamp** lampe (f.)
**land** terre (f.)
**language** langue (f.)
**large** grand
**last** dernier
**late** en retard
**law** loi (f.)
**lawyer** avocat (m.), -e (f.)
**learn** apprendre (irreg.)
**leather** cuir (m.)
**leave (vb.)** partir (irreg.),
  quitter
**lecture** conférence (f.)
**left: on/to the left** à gauche
**leg** jambe (f.)
**less** moins
**lesson** leçon (f.)
**letter** lettre (f.)
**library** bibliothèque (f.)
**life** vie (f.)
**lift** ascenseur (m.)
**like (vb.)** aimer
**listen (to)** écouter
**live** habiter, vivre (irreg.)
**long** long, longue (f.)

**look (at)** regarder
**look for** chercher
**lorry** camion (m.)
**lose** perdre
**loud** fort
**luck** chance (f.)
**luggage** bagages (m. usu.pl.)
**lunch** déjeuner (m.)

**machine** appareil (m.), machine (f.)
**magazine** revue (f.)
**mail** courrier (m.)
**main** principal
**make** faire (irreg.)
**managing director (and chairman)** président-directeur général (m.)
**many** beaucoup (de)
**map** carte (f.), plan (m.)
**market** marché (m.)
**marriage** mariage (m.)
**married** marié
  **to get married** se marier
**match** allumette (f.)
**match (sport)** match (m.)
**match (light)** allumette (f.)
**me** me, moi
**meal** repas (m.)
**meat** viande (f.)
**mechanic** mécanicien (m.)
**medicine** médicament (m.)
**meet** rencontrer
**meeting** réunion (f.)
**message** message (m.)
**method** méthode (f.)
**midday** midi (m.)
**midnight** minuit (m.)
**milk** lait (m.)
**mine** mien (m.), mienne (f.)
**mistake** erreur (f.)
  **to make a mistake** se tromper
**mobile phone** portable (m.)
**modern** moderne
**moment instant,** moment (m.)
**money** argent (m.)
**month** mois (m.)

**mood** humeur (f.)
**more** plus
**morning** matin (m.)
**mother** mère
**motorbike** moto (f.)
**motorist** automobiliste (m. & f.)
**motorway** autoroute (f.)
**mountain** montagne (f.)
**much** beaucoup (de)
  **as much/many** autant (de)
  **so much/many** tant (de)
**museum** musée (m.)
**music** musique (f.)
**must (to have to)** devoir (irreg.)
**my** mon, ma, mes

**name** nom (m.)
**napkin** serviette (f.)
**near** près (adv.) près de (prep.)
**necessary** nécessaire
**neighbour** voisin (m.) -e (f.)
**nephew** neveu
**never** jamais, ne [verb] jamais
**new** neuf, neuve (f.), nouveau
**news** nouvelle(s) (f.)
**newspaper** journal (m.)
**next** prochain
**next to** à côté de
**night** nuit (f.)
**night club** boîte (f.) de nuit
**noise** bruit (m.)
**noisy,** bruyant
**no** non
**no longer** ne [verb] plus
**no one** personne, ne [verb] personne
**normal** normal
**north** nord (m.)
**nose** nez (m.)
**note (message)** petie mot (m.)
**nothing** rien, ne [verb] rien
**now** maintenant
**nuisance: that's a nuisance** c'est énervant
**number** numéro (m.)
**nurse** infirmier (m.), -ière (f.)

**obey** obéir
**obtain** obtenir (irreg.)
**obvious** évident
**occasionally** de temps en temps
**occupied** occupé
**of** de
**odd** bizarre
**offend** offenser
**offer** offre (f.)
**office** bureau
**often** souvent
**oil** huile (f.)
**old** vieux, vieille (f.)
**on** sur
**only** seul, seulement
**open (vb.)** ouvrir (irreg.) j'ouvre,
  nous ouvrons; j'ai ouvert
**open** ouvert
**opera** opéra (m.)
**opinion** avis (m.)
  **in my opinion** à mon avis
**opportunity** occasion (f.)
**opposite** en face (adv.), en face
  de (prep.)
**or** ou
**order (vb.)** commander
  **in order to** pour, afin de
**ordinary** ordinaire
**organise** organiser
**other** autre
**our** notre, nos
**ours** le/la nôtre, les nôtres
**overlook** donner sur
**overtime** heures (f.) supplémentaires

**pack (vb.) (luggage)** faire ses
  valises (f. pl.)
**pain** douleur (f.)
**paint (vb.)** peindre (irreg.)
**park** parc (m.)
**passport** passeport (m.)
**patient** malade (m. & f.)
**pay (for)** payer
**pen** stylo (m.)
**pen (ballpoint)** stylo (m.) bille
**pencil** crayon (m.)

**people** gens (m. pl.)
**perfect (vb.)** perfectionner
**perfume** parfum (m.)
**perhaps** peut-être
**permit (vb.)** permettre (irreg.)
**personal stereo** baladeur (m.)
**persuade** persuader
**photograph** photo (f.)
**photograph (vb.)** prendre
  en photo
**petrol** essence (f.)
**pick up (broadcast)** capter
**pity** dommage (m.)
  **what a pity!** quel dommage!
**plan** projet (m.)
**plane** avion (m.)
**play (vb.)** jouer
**pleasant** agréable
**please** s'il vous plaît
**please (vb.)** plaire (irreg.)
**pleased** content
**pleasure** plaisir (m.)
**pocket** poche (f.)
**policeman** agent de police
**polite** poli
**poor** pauvre
**possible** possible
**postcard** carte (f.) postale
**postman** facteur
**post office** bureau (m.) de poste
**postpone** reporter
**practise** pratiquer
**prefer** préférer
**prepare** préparer
**prescription** ordonnance (f.)
**press** presse (f.)
**press conference** conférence (f.)
  de presse
**pretty** joli
**prevent** empêcher
**price** prix (m.)
**probable** probable
**product** produit (m.)
**profession** profession (f.)
**promise (vb.)** promettre (irreg.)
**psychology** psychologie (f.)

**purse** porte-monnaie (m.)
**put mettre** (irreg.)

**qualifications** diplômes (m. pl.)
**quality** qualité (f.)
**quarrel** dispute (f.)
**quarrel (vb.)** se disputer
**queen** reine
**question** question (f.)
  **to ask a question** poser une
  question
**queue (vb.)** faire la queue
**quick** rapide
**quickly** vite, rapidement
**quiet** calme

**rabies** rage (f.)
**radio** radio (f.)
**railway** station gare (f.)
**rain (vb.)** pleuvoir (irreg.)
  **it is raining** il pleut
  **it rained** il a plu
**rapid** rapide
**rash (skin)** éruption (f.)
**razor** rasoir (m.)
**read** lire (irreg.)
**ready** prêt
**realise** se rendre compte de
**reason** raison (f.)
**reasonable** raisonnable
**receive** recevoir (irreg.) je reçois,
  il reçoit, n. recevons, ils reçoivent;
  j'ai reçu, je recevrai
**recently** récemment
**recommend** recommander
**refuse (vb.)** refuser
**regret (vb.)** regretter
**remember** se souvenir de (irreg.,
  conj. like venir)
**repair (vb.)** réparer
**repeat** répéter
**reply (vb.)** répondre
**reserve** réserver
**rest (vb.)** se reposer
**restaurant** restaurant (m.)
**return (vb.)** retourner, rentrer

**rich** riche
**right** correct
  **on/to the right** à droite
  **to be right** avoir raison
**room** salle (f.)
  **bedroom** chambre (f.)
**Russia** Russie (f.)
**Russian** russe

**sad** triste
**safe (valuables)** coffre-fort (m.)
**sailing: to go sailing** faire de  la voile
**salad** salade (f.)
**salary** salaire (m.)
**sale** vente (f.)
**sales (bargains)** soldes (m. pl.)
**sand** sable (m.)
**say** dire (irreg.)
**Scotland** Écosse (f.)
**Scottish** écossais
**sea** mer (f.)
**seat** place (f.)
**secretary** secrétaire (m. & f.)
**see** voir (irreg.)
**sell** vendre
**send** envoyer (irreg.)
**serious** grave
**serve** servir (irreg.)
**settle** régler
**several** plusieurs
**shave (vb.)** raser, se raser
**shirt** chemise (f.)
**shop** magasin (m.)
**shopkeeper** commercant (m.), -e (f.)
**shopping** courses (f. pl.)
**shop window** vitrine (f.)
**short** court
**show** spectacle (m.)
**show (vb.)** montrer
**shut (vb.)** fermer
**sign (vb.)** signer
**since depuis**; puisque
**sing** chanter
**single (ticket)** aller (m.) simple
  **(room)** chambre (f.) individuelle
  **(unmarried)** célibataire

**single European currency**
  monnaie (f.) unique européenne
**sister** soeur
**sit down** s'asseoir (irreg.)
**size** taille (f.)
**skate (vb.)** patiner
**skating rink** patinoire (f.)
**ski (vb.)** faire du ski
  **water-skiing ski (m.)** nautique
**skirt** jupe (f.)
**sleep (vb.)** dormir (irreg.) je dors,
  il dort, n. dormons; j'ai dormi
**sleeping bag** sac (m.) de couchage
**slowly** lentement
**small** petit
**smart** chic
**smell (vb.)** sentir (irreg.)
**smoke (vb.)** fumer
**snow (vb.)** neiger
**so** si; donc
**some** du (m.), de la (f.)
**something** quelque chose
**son** fils
**soon** bientôt
  **as soon as** aussitôt que
**sorry** désolé
**soup** soupe (f.)
**south** sud (m.)
**Spain** Espagne (f.)
**Spanish** espagnol
**speak** parler
**special offer** promotion (f.)
**spend (money)** dépenser
**spend (time)** passer
**spoon** cuillère (f.)
**sport** sport (m.)
**square** place (f.)
**stamp** timbre (m.)
**start (vb.)** commencer
**station gare,** station (f.)
**stay (vb.)** rester
**still** encore, toujours
**stop** s'arrêter, cesser
**straight** on tout droit
**street** rue (f.)
**street map** plan (m.)
**student** étudiant (m.) ,-e (f.)

**study (vb.)** étudier
**succeed** réussir
**sugar** sucre (m.)
**suit** costume (m.)
**suitcase** valise (f.)
**sun** soleil (m.)
**sunglasses** lunettes (f.) de soleil
**supermarket** supermarché (m.)
**surprise (vb.)** surprendre (irreg.)
**sure** sûr
**survey** enquête (f.)
**swim** nager, se baigner
**swimming pool** piscine (f.)

**tablet** comprimé (m.)
**take** prendre (irreg.)
  **take down** descendre
  **take part** participer
  **take place** avoir lieu
  **take up** monter
**tall** grand
**tea** thé (m.)
**telephone (vb.)** téléphoner
**telephone booth** cabine (f.)
téléphonique
**tell** dire (irreg.)
**tent** tente (f.)
**terrible** affreux
**thank** remercier
**that/this** ce (m.), cette (f.)
**theft** vol (m.)
**their** leur, leurs
**there** là, y
**these/those** ces (m. & f.)
**think** penser
**thirsty, to be thirsty** avoir soif
**ticket** billet (m.)
**time** temps (m.); heure (f.); fois (f.)
**timetable** horaire (m.)
**tip (gratuity)** pourboire (m.)
**tired** fatigué
**today** aujourd'hui
**toilet** toilettes (f. pl.)
**tomorrow** demain
**too** trop
**too much/many** trop (de)
**tooth** dent (f.)

**towel** serviette (f.)
**town** ville (f.)
**train** train (m.)
**translation** traduction (f.)
**travel (vb.)** voyager
**try (vb.)** essayer
**tyre** pneu (m.)

**ugly** laid
**umbrella** parapluie (m.)
**unable: unable to pay** je ne peux pas payer
**under** sous
**understand** comprendre (irreg.)
**unemployed** en/au chômage
**unfair** injuste
**unfortunately** malheureusement
**unhappy** malheureux
**United States** États-Unis (m. pl.)
**until** jusqu'à, jusqu'à ce que
**upstairs** en haut
**usually** d'habitude
**use (vb.)** utiliser

**vacancies (hotel)** chambres libres
**vacate (room)** libérer
**valid** valable
**valuables** objets (m. pl.) de valeur
**vegetable** légume (m.)
**video recorder** magnétoscope (m.)
**view** vue (f.)
  **view over the sea** vue sur mer
**visit (vb.)** visiter

**wait (for)** attendre
**waiter** garçon
**waitress** serveuse
**wake up** réveiller, se réveiller
**Wales** pays (m.) de Galles
**walk (vb.)** marcher
  **to go for a walk** se promener
**wallet** porte-feuille (m.)

**want (vb.)** vouloir (irreg.)
**warm, to be warm** avoir chaud
**wash (vb.)** laver, se laver
**watch (vb.)** regarder
**watch over** surveiller
**watch (wrist)** montre (f.)
**water** eau (f.)
  **drinking water** eau potable
**water-skiing ski (m.) n**autique
**wave** vague (f.)
**wear (vb.)** porter
**week** semaine (f.)
**well** bien
**Welsh** gallois
**west** ouest (m.)
**what** quel (m.), quelle (f.)
**wheel** roue (f.)
**when** quand
**where** où
**which** quel (m.), quelle (f.), que (rel pron.)
**who, whom** qui
**why** pourquoi
**wife** femme
**wind** vent (m.)
**windsurfing** planche (f.) à voile
**wine** vin (m.)
**wish (vb.)** désirer, souhaiter
**wonderful** magnifique
**word** mot (m.)
**work (vb.)** travailler; (of machines) marcher
**write** écrire (irreg.)
**writing paper** papier (m.) à lettres
**wrong: to be wrong** avoir tort

**year** an (m.)
**yesterday** hier
**young** jeune
**your** ton (m. fam.), ta (f. fam.), votre
**yours** le tien (fam.), le vôtre

**accord** (m.) agreement
 **je suis d'accord** I agree
**acheter** to buy
**actrice** actress
**addition** (f.) bill
**adresse** (f.) address
**affaire** (f.) matter
 **c'est une bonne affaire** it's a
 bargain (good buy)
**affaires (f. pl.)** business
 **homme d'a.** businessman
 **femme d'a.** businesswoman
**affreux** dreadful
**afin de** in order to
**agence** (f.) agency
**agréable** pleasant
**aider** to help
**aimable** kind
**aimer** to like, love
**alcool** (m.) alcohol
**Allemagne** (f.) Germany
**allemand** German
**aller (irreg.)** to go
**allumette** (f.) match (light)
**ambassade** (f.) embassy
**ambulance** (f.) ambulance
**ambulancier (m.), -ière** (f.)
**ambulance** driver
**améliorer** to improve
**amener** sec. 81 to bring
**américain** American
**Amérique** (f.) America
**ami (m.), -e (f.)** friend
**amuser** to amuse
 **s'amuser** to enjoy oneself
**an (m.)** year
**analyser** to analyse
**anglais** English
**Angleterre** (f.) England
**annonce** (f.) advertisement
**annoncer** to announce
**annuler** to cancel
**antiquaire (m. & f.)** antique dealer
**appareil (m.)** machine

**appareil-photo (m.)** camera
**appartement (m.)** apartment
**appeler** to call
 **s'appeler** to be called
**apporter** to bring
**apprécier** to appreciate
**apprendre** (irreg.) to learn
**approuver** to approve (of.)
**après** after
**après-midi (m. or f.)** afternoon
**argent (m.)** money
**arrêter, s'arrêter** to stop
**arriver** to arrive; to happen
**ascenseur (m.)** lift, elevator
**asseoir, s'asseoir (irreg.)** to sit
 down
**assez** enough; fairly
**astronaute (m. & f.)** astronaut
**attacher** to attach
**attendre** to wait (for)
**au-dessus de** above
**augmenter** to increase
**augmentation (f.)** increase
**aujourd'hui** today
**au revoir** goodbye
**aussi** also
**aussitôt que** as soon as
**autant (de)** as much/many
**autobus (m.)** bus
**automobiliste (m. & f.)** motorist
**autoroute (f.)** motorway
**autre** other
**avance: à l'avance** in advance
**avant** before
**avion (m.)** aeroplane
**avis (m.)** opinion
 **à mon avis** in my opinion
**avocat (m.), -e (f.)** lawyer
**avoir (irreg.)** to have
 **avoir lieu** to take place

**bagages (m. pl.)** luggage
**baigner: se b.** to have a swim
**bain (m.)** bath

**baladeur (m.)** personal stereo, Walkman
**banque (f.)** bank
**banquier (m.), -ière (f.)** banker
**bar (m.)** bar
**bas, basse (f.)** low
  **en bas** downstairs
**bateau (m.)** boat
**beau** beautiful
**beaucoup (de)** much/many
**Belgique (f.)** Belgium
**bibliothèque (f.)** library
**bicyclette (f.)** bicycle
**bien** well
**bien que (+subj)** although
**bientôt** soon
**bière (f.)** beer
**bilingue** bilingual
**billet (m.)** ticket
**bizarre** odd
**blessé** injured
**bleu** blue
**boire (irreg.)** to drink
**boîte (f.)** box
  **boite de nuit** nightclub
**bon, bonne (f.)** good
**boucherie (f.)** butcher's
**boulangerie (f.)** baker's
**bouteille (f.)** bottle
**bras (m.)** arm
**britannique** British
**brochure (f.)** brochure
**brouillard (m.)** fog
**bruit (m.)** noise
**brûler** to burn
**brun** brown
**bruyant** noisy

**cadeau (m.)** gift
**café (m.)** coffee; café
**caisse (f.)** cashdesk
**calme** calm, quiet
**cambrioleur (m.)** burglar
**camion (m.)** lorry

**camper** to camp
**Canada (m.)** Canada
**capter** to pick up (broadcast)
**car (m.)** coach
**carte (f.)** card; map
**carte de crédit** credit card
**carte postale** postcard
**casser** to break
**cathédrale (f.)** cathedral
**ce, cette, etc** this
**celui, celle, etc** the one
**célèbre** famous
**cesser** to stop
**chaise (f.)** chair
**chaise longue** deckchair
**chambre (f.)** bedroom
**femme de chambre** chambermaid
**champ (m.)** field
**chance (f.)** luck
**changer** to change
**chanter** to sing
**chapeau (m.)** hat
**chaque** each
**château (m.)** castle
**chaud** hot
  **avoir chaud** to be hot, warm
  **il fait c.** it's warm (weather)
**chemise (f.)** shirt
**chemise de nuit** nightshirt
**chèque (m.)** cheque
**cher (m.), chère (f.)** dear
**chercher** to look for
**cheveux (m. pl.)** hair (on head)
**chic (inv)** smart
**Chine (f.)** China
**choisir** to choose
**chômage (m.)** unemployment
**en/au chômage** unemployed
**clé (f.)** key
**client (m.), -e (f.)** customer
**climatisation (f.)** air-conditioning
**cœur (m.)** heart
**coffre-fort (m.)** safe (box)
**coiffeur (m.), -euse (f.)** hairdresser

**combien** how much/many
**commander** to order
**commencer** to begin
**comment** how
**commerçant (m.), -e(f.)** shopkeeper
**compagnie (f.) aérienne** airline company
**composer (un numéro)** to dial
**comprendre (irreg.)** to understand
**comprimé (m.)** tablet
**compris** included
**conduire (irreg.)** to drive
**conférence (f.)** conference; lecture
**confirmer** to confirm
**confiture (f.)** jam
**confortable** comfortable
**connaître (irreg.)** to know
**conseiller** to advise
**construire (irreg.)** to build
**consulter** to consult
**content** pleased
**continuer** to continue
**contrat (m.)** contract
**copier** to copy
**correct** correct
**corriger** to correct
**costume (m.)** suit
**côté (m.)** side
  **à côté de** next to
**couleur (f.)** colour
**couper** to cut
**courageux** brave
**courrier (m.)** mail
**courses (f. pl.)** shopping
**court** short
**couteau (m.)** knife
**coûter** to cost
**crayon (m.)** pencil
**créer** to create
**critiquer** to criticise
**cuillère (f.)** spoon
**cuir (m.)** leather

**cuisine (f.)** kitchen; cooking

**dame** lady
**dangereux** dangerous
**danser** to dance
**date (f.)** date
**débarquer** to disembark
**décider** to decide
**décourager** to discourage
**défendre** to defend; to forbid
**déjà** already
**déjeuner (m.)** lunch
  **petit déjeuner** breakfast
**délicieux** delicious
**demain** tomorrow
**demander** to ask (for)
**dent (f.)** tooth
**dentiste (m. & f.)** dentist
**départ (m.)** departure
**dépêcher, se d.** to hurry
**dépenser** to spend (money)
**depuis** since
**déranger** to disturb
**dernier** last
**derrière** behind
**descendre** to go down; to take down
**désirer** to wish
**désolé** sorry
**détester** to hate
**devant** in front of
**devoir (irreg.)** to have to (must)
**dictionnaire (m.)** dictionary
**difficile** difficult
**diner (m.)** dinner
**diplôme (m.)** diploma
**dire (irreg.)** to say, tell
**directeur (m.), -trice (f.)** director
**discothèque (f.)** disco
**discuter de** to discuss
**dispute (f.)** quarrel
  **se disputer** to quarrel
**disque (m.)** record
**disquette (f.)** floppy disk

**distractions (f. pl.)** entertainment
**docteur (m.)** doctor
**dommage: quel dommage** what
  a pity
**donc** so, therefore
**donner** to give
**donner sur** to overlook (view)
**dormir (irreg.)** to sleep
  **je dors, il dort, n. dormons,**
  **j'ai dormi**
**douane (f.)** customs
**douanier (m.), -ière (f.)** customs
officer
**douleur (f.)** pain
**douter** to doubt
**drapeau (m.)** flag
**droit: tout droit** straight on
**droite: à droite** on/to the right
**du, de la, etc.** sec. 1 some

**eau (f.)** water
  **eau potable** drinking water
**écossais** Scottish
**Écosse (f.)** Scotland
**écouter** to listen (to)
**écrire (irreg.)** to write
**écriture (f.)** handwriting
**efficace** efficient
**église (f.)** church
**électricien (m.)** electrician
**émission (f.)** broadcast
**empêcher** to prevent
**emploi (m.)** job
**encore** again; still; yet
**encourager** to encourage
**énervant** annoying
**ennuyeux** boring; annoying
  **s'ennuyer** to be bored
**enquête (f.)** survey
**ensuite** afterwards
**entendre** to hear
**entre** between
**entrer** to enter
**enveloppe (f.)** envelope

**envoyer (irreg.)** to send
**épicerie (f.)** food store
**erreur (f.)** mistake
**éruption (f.)** rash (skin)
**Espagne (f.)** Spain
**espagnol** Spanish
**espérer** to hope
**essayer** to try
**essence (f.)** petrol
**est (m.)** east
**et** and
**États-Unis (m. pl.)** United States
**étranger** foreign
  **à l'étranger** abroad
**être (irreg.)** to be
**étudiant (m.), -e (f.)** student
**étudier** to study
**évident** obvious
**éviter** to avoid
**exactement** exactly
**excellent** excellent
**excursion (f.)** excursion
**explication (f.)** explanation
**exporter** to export

**face: en face de** opposite
**facile** easy
**facteur (m.), -trice (f.)** postman/
  postwoman
**facture (f.)** invoice
**faim (f.)** hunger
  **avoir faim** to be hungry
**faire (irreg.)** to do, make
**falloir (irreg.)** to be necessary; need
**il nous faut partir** we must leave;
**il nous faut 50 euros** we need 50
  euros
**famille (f.)** family
**fatigué** tired
**faut** see falloir
**fauteuil (m.)** armchair
**féliciter** to congratulate
**femme** woman; wife
**fermer** to shut

fièvre (f.) fever
fille daughter
  jeune fille girl
film (m.) film
fils son
fin (f.) end
finir to finish
fois (f.) time (occasion)
fort strong; loud
fourchette (f.) fork
frais (m.) fraîche (f.) fresh
français French
France (f.) France
frapper to knock
frère brother
froid cold
  avoir froid to be cold
  il fait f. it's cold (weather)
fromage (m.) cheese
fruit(s) (m.) fruit
fumer to smoke

gagner to win; earn
gallois Welsh
gant (m.) glove
garage (m.) garage
garantir to guarantee
garçon boy; waiter
garder to keep
gare (f.) railway station
gâteau (m.) cake
gauche: à gauche on/to the left
généralement generally
gens (m. pl.) people
glace (f.) ice; ice cream
gouvernement (m.) government
grand big, tall
Grande-Bretagne (f.) Britain
grave serious
Grèce (f.) Greece
gris grey
groupe (m.) group
guide (m.) guide; guidebook

habiter to live
habitude (f.) habit
d'habitude usually
haut high
  en haut upstairs
heure (f.) hour
  heures supplémentaires
  overtime
heureux happy
heureusement fortunately
hier yesterday
homme man
hôpital (m.) hospital
horaire (m.) timetable
hôtel (m.) hotel
huile (f.) oil
humeur (f.) mood
ici here
il y a there is/are; ago
important important
importer to import
impossible impossible
impressionnant impressive
incendie (m.) fire
infirmier (m.), -ière (f.) nurse
ingénieur (m.) engineer
injuste unfair
instant (m.) moment
intéressant interesting
interprète (m. & f.) interpreter
inviter to invite
irlandais Irish
Irlande (f.) Ireland

jamais, ne [verb] jamais never
jambe (f.) leg
jambon (m.) ham
Japon (m.) Japan
japonais Japanese
jardin (m.) garden
jeune young
joli pretty
jouer to play
journal (m.) newspaper

journaliste (m. & f.) journalist
jupe (f.) skirt
jusqu'à as far as; until

là there
lac (m.) lake
laid ugly
lait (m.) milk
lampe (f.) lamp
langue (f.) tongue; language
laver to wash
se laver to wash oneself
leçon (f.) lesson
légume vegetable
lentement slowly
lettre (f.) letter
leur their
le leur theirs
lever to raise
se lever to get up
libérer to free, vacate
librairie (f.) bookshop
libre free
licence (f.) degree (univ.)
lire (irreg.) to read
lit (m.) bed
livre (m.) book
livre (f.) pound
logiciel (m.) software (comput.)
loi (f.) law
loin far long,
long (m.), longue (f.) long
louer to hire
lourd heavy
lunettes (f. pl.) spectacles
  lunettes de soleil sunglasses

machine (f.) machine
magasin (m.) shop
magnétoscope (m.) video recorder
magnifique wonderful
main (f.) hand
maintenant now
mais but

maison (f.) house
mal badly
malade ill
maladie (f.) illness
  malade de la 'vache folle'
  'mad cow' disease
malheureux unhappy
malheureusement unfortunately
Manche (f.) Channel
manger to eat
marchander to haggle
marché (m.) market
Marché commun Common Market
marcher to walk
mari husband
mariage (m.) marriage
marié married
marier: se marier to get married
marque (f.) brand
match (m.) match (sport)
matin (m.) morning
mauvais bad
mécanicien (m.) mechanic
médecin (m.) doctor
médicament (m.) medicine
meilleur (adj.) better
même same; even
mer (f.) sea
mère mother
message (m.) message
méthode (f.) method
mettre (irreg.) to put
midi (m.) midday
mien, le mien mine
mieux better
minuit (m.) midnight
mode (f.) fashion
moderne modern
moi me
  avec/pour moi with/for me
moins less
mois (m.) month
moitié (f.) half
mon, ma, mes my

montagne (f.) mountain
monter to go up; take up
montre (f.) watch
montrer to show
mouchoir (m.) handkerchief
mot (m.) word
  un petit mot a note
moteur (m.) engine
moto (f.) motorbike
musée (m.) museum
musique (f.) music

nager to swim
nécessaire necessary
neiger to snow
nettoyer to clean
neuf (m.), neuve (f.) new
neveu nephew
nez (m.) nose
nièce niece
nom (m.) name
non no
nord (m.) north
normal normal
note (f.) bill
notre, nos our
  le nôtre ours
nourriture (f.) food
nouveau new
nouvelle(s) (f.) news
nuit (f.) night
  boîte (f.) de nuit nightclub
numéro (m.) number

obéir to obey
obtenir (irreg.) to obtain
occasion (f.) opportunity
  une voiture d'o. a used car
occupé busy
offenser to offend
offre (f.) offer
opéra (m.) opera
ordinaire ordinary
ordinateur (m.) computer

ordonnance (f.) prescription
organiser to organise
ou or
où where
oublier to forget
ouest (m.) west
ouvrir (irreg.) to open
  j'ouvre, il ouvre, n. ouvrons,
  j'ai ouvert
ouvert (adj.) open

pain (m.) bread
pain grillé toast
panne (f.) breakdown
papier (m.) paper
papier à lettres writing paper
parapluie (m.) umbrella
parc (m.) park
parce que because
pardonner to forgive
parfum (m.) perfume
parler to speak
participer to take part
partir (irreg.) to leave
partout everywhere
passeport (m.) passport
passer to spend (time)
patiner to skate
patinoire (f.) skating rink
patron (m.), -onne (f.) owner, boss
pauvre poor
payer to pay (for)
  p. en espèces to pay in cash
pays (m.) country
pays (m.) de Galles Wales
pêche (f.) peach
pêche (f.) fishing
  aller à la pêche to go fishing
peindre (irreg.) to paint
pellicule (f.) film (for snapshots)
penser to think
perdre to lose
père father
perfectionner to perfect

**permettre (irreg.)** to allow
**permis (m.)** licence
  **p. de conduire** driving licence
**personne (f.)** person
**ne [verb] personne** no-one
**persuader** to persuade
**petit** small
**peut-être** perhaps
**pharmacie (f.)** chemist's
**photo (f.)** photograph
  **prendre en p.** to take a photo
**pièce (f.) d'identité** identification
**piscine (f.)** swimming pool
**place (f.)** place, seat; square
**plage (f.)** beach
**plainte (f.)** complaint
**plaire (irreg.)** to please
**s'il vous plaît** please
**plaisir (m.)** pleasure
**plan (m.)** street map
**planche (f.) à voile** windsurfing
  board
  **faire de la planche à voile**
  to windsurf
**plat (m.)** dish
**platine laser (f.)** CD player
**plein** full
**pleuvoir (irreg.)** to rain
  **il pleut** it's raining
  **il a plu** it rained
**plonger** to dive
**plus** more
**ne [verb] plus** no more/no longer
**plusieurs** several
**pneu (m.)** tyre
**poche (f.)** pocket
**poisson (m.)** fish
**poissonnerie (f.)** fishmonger's
**poli** polite
**police (f.)** police
  **un agent de police** policeman
**pomme (f.)** apple
**pomme de terre** potato
**pompier (m.)** fireman

**port (m.)** port, harbour
**portable (m.)** mobile phone
**porte-feuille (m.)** wallet
**porte-monnaie (m.)** purse
**porter** to carry; wear
**possible** possible
**poste (m.)** job
**poste (f.)** post office
**pour** for; in order to
**pourboire (m.)** tip (gratuity)
**pourquoi** why
**pouvoir (irreg.)** to be able (can)
**pratiquer** to practise
**préférer** to prefer
**premier** first
**prendre (irreg.)** to take
**préparer** to prepare
**près de** near
**président-directeur général**
  chairman and managing director
**presse (f.)** press
  **conférence de presse**
  press conference
**prêt** ready
**principal** main
**prix (m.)** price
**probable** probable
**prochain** next
**produit (m.)** product
**profession (f.)** profession
**profond** deep
**projet (m.)** plan
**promener** sec. 81 to take for a walk
**se promener** to go for a walk
**promettre (irreg.)** to promise
**promotion (f.)** special offer
**psychologie (f.)** psychology
**publicité (f.)** advertising
**puisque** since, because

**qualité (f.)** quality
**quand** when
**que (interrog)** what
**que (rel. pron.)** whom/which

**quel** which/what
**quelque** chose something
**question (f.)** question
  **poser une question** to ask a
  question
**queue (f.)** queue
  **faire la queue** to queue
**qui (interrog)** who
**qui (rel. pron.)** who/which
**quitter** to leave
**quoique (+ subj)** although

**radio (f.)** radio
**rage (f.)** rabies
**raison (f.)** reason
  **avoir raisin** to be right
**raisonnable** reasonable
**rapidement** quickly
**raser** to shave
  **se raser** to shave oneself
**rasoir (m.)** razor
**récemment** recently
**recevoir (irreg.)** to receive
  **je reçois, il reçoit, nous**
  **recevons, ils reçoivent, j'ai**
  **reçu, je recevrai**
**recommender** to recommend
**refuser** to refuse
**regarder** to look (at), watch
**régime (m.)** diet
**régler** to settle
**regretter** to regret
**reine** queen
**remercier** to thank
**remplir** to fill
**rencontrer** to meet
**rendez-vous (m.)** appointment
**rendre** to give back
**renseignment(s)** information
**rentrer** to return
**réparer** to repair
**repas (m.)** meal
**répéter** to repeat
**répondre** to reply

**reporter (m.)** reporter (news)
**reporter** to take back;
  postpone
**reposer, se reposer** to rest
**réserver** to book
**restaurant (m.)** restaurant
**rester** to stay
**retard (m.)** lateness
  **en retard** late
**retourner** to return
**réunion (f.)** meeting
**réussir** to succeed
**réveiller, se réveiller** to wake up
**revenu (m.)** income
**revue (f.)** magazine
**rhume (m.)** cold
  **rhume des foins** hayfever
**riche** rich
**rien: ne [verb] rien** nothing
**robe (f.)** dress
**roue (f.)** wheel
**rouler** to drive
**rue (f.)** street
**russe** Russian
**Russie (f.)** Russia

**sable (m.)** sand
**sac (m.)** bag
**sac à main** handbag
**sac de couchage** sleeping bag
**salade (f.)** salad
**salaire (m.)** salary
**sale** dirty
**salle (f.)** room
**santé (f.)** health
**savoir (irreg.)** to know
**secrétaire (m. & f.)** secretary
**semaine (f.)** week
**serveuse** waitress
**serviette (f.)** napkin; towel;
  briefcase
**servir (irreg.)** to serve
**seul** alone; only
**seulement** only

**sida (m.)** AIDS
**sien, le sien** his/hers/its
**signer** to sign
**ski (m.)** skiing
  **ski nautique** water-skiing
  **faire du ski** to go skiing
**sœur** sister
**soif (f.)** thirst
  **avoir soif** to be thirsty
**soir (m.)** evening
**soldes (m. pl.)** sales (bargains)
**soleil (m.)** sun
**lunettes (f. pl.) de soleil** sunglasses
**son, sa, ses** his/her/its
**sortie (f.)** exit
  **sortie de secours** fire exit
**sortir (irreg.)** to go out;
  take out
**souhaiter** to wish
**soupe (f.)** soup
**sous** under
**souvenir (m.)** souvenir; memory
**se souvenir de (conj. like venir)**
  to remember
**souvent** often
**spectacle (m.)** show
**sport (m.)** sport
**stylo (m.)** pen
  **stylo bille** ballpoint pen
**sucre (m.)** sugar
**sud (m.)** south
**supermarché (m.)** supermarket
**supplément (m.)** extra
**sur** on
**sûr** sure
**surprendre (irreg.)** to surprise
**surtout** especially
**surveiller** to watch over
**taille (f.)** size; waist
**tant (de)** so much/many
**tante** aunt
**tasse (f.)** cup
**télégramme (m.)** telegram
**téléphone (m.)** telephone

**téléphoner** to telephone
  **cabine téléphonique** telephone
  booth
**temps (m.)** time
  **de temps en temps** occasionally
**tension (f.)** stress; blood pressure
**tente (f.)** tent
**terre (f.)** land
**tête (f.)** head
**thé (m.)** tea
**tien, le tien** yours
**timbre (m.)** stamp
**toilettes (f. pl.)** toilet
**tomber** to fall
  **t. en panne** to break down
**ton, ta, tes** your

**tort: avoir tort** to be wrong
**tôt** early
**toujours** always; still
**tout** all
**tout le monde** everyone
**tout de suite** immediately
**tout** everything
**traduction (f.)** translation
**train (m.)** train
**travailler** to work
**traverser** to cross
**triste** sad
**tromper** to deceive
**se tromper** to make a mistake
**trop** too
**trop (de)** too much/many
**trouver** to find

**Union (f.) européenne**
  European Union
**urgence (f.)** emergency
**en cas d'urgence** in an emergency
**utiliser** to use
**vacances (f. pl.)** holidays
**vague (f.)** wave
**valable** valid
**valeur (f.)** value

**objets de valeur** valuables
**valise (f.)** suitcase
**faires ses valises** to pack
**vélo (m.)** bike
**vendre** to sell
**venir (irreg.)** to come
**vent (m.)** wind
**vente (f.)** sale
**vérifier** to check
**verre (m.)** glass
**verser** to pour; pay
**verser des arrhes (f. pl.)** to leave
  a deposit
**veste (f.)** jacket
**vestibule (m.)** hall
**vêtements (m. pl.)** clothes
**viande (f.)** meat
**vie (f.)** life

**vieux** old
**ville (f.)** town
**vin (m.)** wine
**visiter** to visit
**vitrine (f.)** shop window
**vivre (irreg.)** to live
**voici** here is/are
**voile (f.)** sail
  **faire de la voile** to go sailing
**voir (irreg.)** to see
**voisin (m.), -e (f.)** neighbour
**voiture (f.)** car
**vol (m.)** flight; theft
**vôtre** your
**vôtre, le vôtre** yours
**vouloir (irreg.)** to want
**voyager** to travel
**vue (f.)** view

# Index

The numbers refer to section headings, unless pages are specified